The Writing Puzzle

Madeleine Scalliet Waters

*San Bernadino
Valley College*

Second Edition

KENDALL/HUNT PUBLISHING COMPANY
4050 Westmark Drive   Dubuque, Iowa 52002

Contents

3

Sentence Imitation: Understanding Structure and Developing Vocabulary   35

4

Phrase Combining: From Random Thoughts to Polished Paragraphs   127

 # Preface

The rationale for the approach to teaching basic writing skills described in this text can be summarized as follows:

- Sentence-based instruction with very little formal grammar provides opportunities for writing improvements that occur faster and with more enjoyment than with traditional methods.
- The Writing Puzzle method taps on students' current knowledge of language, spoken and written; it gives it formality and precision of meaning; it changes bad writing habits into good ones.
- The method consists of guiding students through an imitation technique of excellent sentence models while they provide their own content.
- Once students internalize many excellent sentence patterns, they move into a freer mode of composition.
- Higher-level thinking skills based on *how* and *why* questions become embedded in the sentence structure.
- A natural phenomenon occurs where accurate writing stimulates accurate and precise thinking, and precise thinking, in turn, maintains accurate writing.

This method is designed to help everyone. It is completely versatile and provides skill-building opportunities and strategies for writers of any age and at any level of previous knowledge. Its versatility also makes it successful with students whose native language is not English.

Preface to the Second Edition

It has been rewarding to work with the first edition of this text and to accumulate in-the-field evidence of its success. However, its use in the classroom has also brought into light the need for improvements in the presentation and for additional material.

This edition moves the grammatical reference from the back of the text to the front in the first chapter. This change is important because the grammatical information is limited to a description of the parts of speech, yet it represents necessary knowledge before correct imitation of sentence models can take place. Since the parts of speech represent the raw materials used for sentence construction, they must be learned in order to identify them in the structure of a sentence and imitate that structure.

Another change in the second edition is a set of user friendly templates in Chapter 2. These tools translate the grammatical information of Chapter 1 into quick and handy reference pages.

In the sentence imitation chapter, Chapter 3, sentence models have been organized into categories based on the types of sentences, from simple to compound/complex. Many models have been added. These models are divided into workshops as this is a book that must be used as a workbook. In addition, the first workshop gives a complete diagram for the structure of each sentence model. This addition introduces the student to the necessary step of dissecting sentences before imitating them.

Another addition to Chapter 3 is a sample imitation of each sentence model provided to the student as an example of correct imitation. Students rarely do sentence imitation, and they often have difficulty moving away from the model and thinking of something different to say while keeping the same structure. Occasionally, students do sentence copying instead of sentence imitation. An example of correct sentence imitation gets them started in the right direction.

Finally, the list of topic suggestions for paragraphs and short essays has been lengthened.

I know that these changes and additions will enhance the effectiveness of this writing method. Any textbook, however, remains a work in progress. I welcome all users to let me know what works for them and what they would like to see in the book. They can reach me at the Kendall/Hunt Publishing website www.kendallhunt.com or write to me directly at Madeleine_waters@redlands.edu.

 Acknowledgments

I thank all my students who were the first ones to use this book and learn from it. They showed me all that could be improved and added and have contributed greatly to this second edition. I also thank my colleagues in the field of English who have shared their classroom experiences and have encouraged me to work on this revision.

Madeleine Scalliet Waters

Introduction to the Instructor

During my many years of teaching basic grammar in community colleges and universities, I have cried for my students, I have cried with my students, and I have cried for myself! I have constantly searched for a better text, I have incessantly looked for more effective presentation methods, and I have often gone home wondering what was wrong with the students . . . or with me.

Over time, I have established that:

- The quality of students' writing is poor, but the pressures for writing excellence are high.
- Systematic grammar instruction is time-consuming and rarely effective.
- One reason for its lack of effectiveness is students' inability to focus on and understand the language of grammar.
- Another reason is the lack of transfer from memorized grammatical rules to applications in composition.

The students who take mandatory writing classes in order to earn a degree often experience incredible pain, self-doubt, and despair. Many give up early. Some are satisfied with a passing grade without devoting much time to improving their existing skills. A few memorize the material and get good scores on quizzes, but they rarely apply this new knowledge in their compositions.

Does it really matter? Yes, of course. Writing well and speaking clearly are essential skills to be effective in life. But is it necessary to learn innumerable grammatical terms and their definitions? I used to think so. I now see that, as some people play beautiful music without reading the notes, others write well without the benefit of formal grammar instruction. All students, at any level of desire or ability, can have access to techniques and strategies that will transform their writing from incoherence to clarity with or without formal grammar instruction.

THE WRITING PUZZLE METHOD

The Writing Puzzle approach to instruction in composition provides students with rules for sentence structure and punctuation with very little formal grammar instruction. Those who meet the learning objectives of the Writing Puzzle will:

- Improve their writing skills generally.
- Expand their vocabulary.
- Develop confidence in their writing abilities and the readability of their compositions.
- Acquire disciplined writing practice.

- Recognize the options available to writers.
- Learn the most appropriate choices for clarity, accuracy, and precision.
- Assimilate a direct writing approach that will transfer to all types of writing assignments.
- Discover how to control language for writing effectiveness.

These learning objectives need not translate into lengthy and intense instructional goals. The curriculum is simple and based on the following conclusions to classroom-based observations:

- The reality in writing classes is that the *run-on sentence*, the *comma splice*, and the *fragment* have taken over composition.
- The purpose of writing is to be read, understood, and enjoyed. This requires clarity, accuracy, precision, and a varied vocabulary.
- No paragraph will achieve these characteristics unless each sentence within it is clear, accurate, precise, and interesting.
- Clarity, accuracy, precision, and interest require detail and sentence length with articulations that support meaning.
- *Punctuation* and *conjunctions* provide sentence articulation, and they control the majority of variations in meaning; therefore, accurate meaning is created at the sentence level.
- These parameters for meaning can only be held in working memory at the sentence level.

This short writing method is intended to help students of any age and ability who have difficulty learning the parts of speech and understanding how they are used in sentences. Although deceivingly simple, it requires discipline and absolute precision in imitating sentence models. When correctly applied, it will rapidly give students a sense of personal mastery over their written output. The method teaches little grammar, but it provides grammatical references and small capsules of grammatical instruction. Spelling issues are not addressed directly, but strict imitation of given models includes absolute correctness in spelling. Punctuation issues are addressed as they appear in the various sentence models. The method targets writing at the sentence level, the most fundamental unit in composing paragraphs and essays. I believe that mastering the art of writing clear, correct, and varied sentences, one at a time, necessarily leads to composing good paragraphs and, ultimately, good and interesting essays.

THE BARRIERS TO LEARNING GRAMMAR

For many students, barriers exist to learning grammar and using it effectively in writing. Whatever these barriers may be, they must be eliminated, but instruction must not become so simplified that it also becomes useless. Many students tell me how confusing grammar books can be when they use several terms to name the same thing. For example, instead of learning the term *linking verb* and understanding what it refers to with examples, students must also remember that, in some texts, a *linking verb* is called a *state of being verb*. Similarly, a *helping verb* is also called an *auxiliary verb*. They now have to remember that both terms refer to the same thing! In an attempt to simplify the material, we often create confusion and remain ineffective.

Here are observations from the classroom regarding barriers to learning:

- A strong resistance exists against thinking about the language we use.
- Habits of language take a strong hold. They seem to support the desire to avoid clarity and precision in verbal exchanges.
- Writers take little responsibility in the level of readability of their output.
- Many writers have not acquired the study skills and the vocabulary needed to learn grammar effectively.
- It is the understanding of the components of sentences and the dynamics that exist between them that is painful and very difficult for many to learn.

Most adult students who sit in a grammar class feel that they are trying to learn a foreign language, mostly because they are asked to speak and write formally. I have long believed that this could only be achieved with the study of grammar. I now prefer to capitalize on the existing knowledge students have of their language in its everyday use, and to expose them to a more formal and accurate version of it as well as to more options for conveying meaning.

THE VALUE OF IMITATION

Learning theorists like Piaget and Bandura emphasize the role of imitation and models in young children's learning. Young and adult students can learn good writing by imitating structures given to them as models until their imitation becomes second nature. Then, they can shift into a creative mode in which they no longer have a model sentence on paper. They create their own, tapping on the resources of structures previously learned through imitation. This approach is based on the following:

- Imitation is an automatic learning style.
- The richer the environment, the busier we get at imitating. In writing classes, the environment is often poor for lack of excellent sentence models on which students can focus their attention.
- An excellent sentence includes precise and interesting vocabulary as well as accurate structure to support meaning.
- The more excellent sentence models that are provided for imitation, the larger the bank of writing options available for good writing after one has internalized the patterns first imitated.
- The more one becomes aware of the large variety of excellent sentence structures, the more one wishes to expand and explore, slowly substituting one's personal style for direct imitation while retaining the structures that ensure clarity, accuracy, and precision.

Behavioral specialists know that new habits are acquired in approximately four weeks. This represents roughly one third of a semester-long course and the amount of time instructors should confine themselves to teaching the imitation stage. During this stage, absolute correctness in reproducing sentence structures, punctuation, and spelling is essential. The second stage, based on the Jigsaw Puzzle model, expands into a freer and more creative writing mode while using the resources of the sentence database built through imitation and repetition. Its techniques are illustrated in the fourth chapter of this text.

THE JIGSAW PUZZLE MODEL FOR PARAGRAPH CONSTRUCTION

A piece of writing evokes a picture in the reader's mind, so I have selected the Jigsaw Puzzle model for this second stage in learning to write well. It can be broken down into the following steps:

- The first step consists of making lists of the things one wants to say and using short phrases to do so. This list becomes the equivalent of the edge pieces of the puzzle. It sets the content and meaning parameters of the piece of writing.
- The short phrases answer the questions *who, what, when, where, how,* and *why*.
- The second step is to organize the short phrases by ranking them in order of importance and in order of relationships between ideas. This is like making separate piles of puzzle pieces according to color or shape.
- Finally, one must collect the nuts-and-bolts type words and symbols used for articulating sentences, like prepositions, conjunctions, and punctuation marks. They will make the pieces fit together perfectly into pleasant, correct, and well-articulated sentences.

LIST MAKING AND PHRASE COMBINING

The type of list that best fulfills a writer's needs is a list of very short phrases, which break down the bulk of the information into small units to be assembled into effective sentences.

The advantages of such lists are:

- They help writers meet their biggest challenge, which is to bridge the gap from bulk information to polished sentences.
- They give a fast visual take of the completeness and accuracy of the information.
- They also provide for fast organization into ranking order and relationship order. The ranking order determines which facts should be presented first. The relationship order indicates how the facts or ideas are connected to each other as in cause and effect or contrast.
- These short phrases must then be assembled into longer, well-structured sentences.

With the previous practice in imitation, this method makes writing easier.

HOW TO USE THIS BOOK

This text suits best the workshop approach. It should be used as a practice (Chapter 4) and reference tool (Chapters 1 and 2), as well as a means of providing instruction capsules with Chapter 3, which is devoted to sentence imitation. Although some sentences may seem too easy to some, they will not be easy if students do not recognize in them the parts of speech used in the sentence structure. Correct imitation requires that when a noun is used in the model, a noun is also used in the imitation. When an irregular verb in the past tense is used in the model, an irregular verb in the past tense must be used in the imitation. If an adverb is used in the model, an adverb must also be used in the imitation. No matter how short and simple a sentence is, it might not be imitated correctly if the student does not recognize these parts of speech. All students will occasionally need guidance in recognizing certain types of words and learning to discriminate between the parts of speech, the raw materials of sentence construction.

Although the use of this book requires little grammatical instruction, instructors have an opportunity to address various grammatical issues that explain errors when they occur in the reproduction of sentence models. The instructor will decide what level of complexity in the explanation is appropriate for the student who made the error.

The instructor will also decide when errors in one student's work will benefit the entire class. On these occasions, small teaching capsules will be delivered to the entire group. Students generally give their permission to have their work used as a learning tool. An important aspect of teaching with this method is to anonymously read students' sentences aloud. Instructors must *perform* the sentences frequently, giving appropriate tone, emphasis, and pauses. These readings are intricately bound to the production of correct sentence construction and punctuation.

Once students understand this method, they start showing great enthusiasm for it, and they develop a desire to compete with themselves and with others. They soon thrive on the structure given to their writing efforts. It is important to have students write many small paragraphs even while they are learning to imitate sentence structures so they can slowly transfer new learning into the paragraph. After writing their first perfect paragraph, they will often revert back to making errors in their second one. They need to continue writing with great concentration before they become consistent in their good results.

In Chapter 3, space for imitation is given after each sentence model. Students, however, must use a notebook at all times and fill it with more sentence practices, making sure that they identify each time which structure they are imitating by copying and underlining the model first. Under the underlined model sentence, they will write their imitations of it. The key to obtaining the greatest benefit from sentence imitation is to change the words but keep the structure of the sentence. In some sentence models, a specific word must be retained in the imitation because it is the target of the lesson. This is clearly indicated at the beginning of each workshop. Otherwise, students must choose their own content, not only to make the imitation exercise worthwhile but also to expand their vocabulary. The models are organized in groups of sentences from simple to complex.

The models for imitation practice represent the essential foundation for future expansion of students' writing. Therefore, ***it is imperative that plenty of time be given to this stage and that the rule of absolute correctness be imposed at all times.***

1

RAW MATERIALS FOR SENTENCE CONSTRUCTION: THE PARTS OF SPEECH

In order to build a wall or a house, you need to be completely familiar with the materials available to complete the project, and then choose among them to achieve a certain look and a specific use.

Likewise, to write successfully, you must also be well acquainted with the materials available to construct sentences so that they carry the intended meanings. All words in the language, the raw materials, are divided into eight categories called the *parts of speech*: nouns, pronouns, adjectives, verbs, adverbs, prepositions, conjunctions, and interjections. These names become relevant when the words are used in sentences where each one takes on a specific function and must follow specific grammatical and punctuation rules. In order to construct correct sentences, it is then necessary to learn how to identify the parts of speech, understand their function in the sentence, and practice the application of punctuation and grammatical rules that go along with that function. Complications come about from the fact that words sometimes take on more than one function. For example, nouns can be used as adjectives or prepositions can be used as conjunctions. This is why the definition of the parts of speech must be learned very well so that their true function in a sentence is easily identified and rules that apply to that function are followed.

Although this writing method minimizes grammatical instruction, it cannot eliminate a lesson on the parts of speech. In this chapter, you will learn what the parts of speech are and what rules they follow in many types of sentences. When you understand this lesson, memorize some of the information. When you can accurately identify the parts of speech most of the time, move to sentence imitation in Chapter 3.

THE NOUN

Nouns are plentiful. They are used to name the *things* that surround us, the *people* around us, the *places* we go to, and also the *ideas* that come to our mind.

- When nouns are used for specific places, they are capitalized.

  EXAMPLE

  Las Vegas

- When nouns are used as people's names, they are capitalized.

  EXAMPLE

  Mrs. Thompson

- Nouns are singular or plural according to how many of the things, places, people, or ideas you talk about. When used in the plural, nouns typically take an *s*. However, some nouns have an irregular plural form.

  EXAMPLES

Regular plural:	one tree	two trees
Irregular plurals:	one man	three men
	one box	five boxes
	one brush	ten brushes
	one mouse	a hundred mice

This is clearly not a complete list of all irregular nouns. If you are in doubt about the plural form of a noun, consult your dictionary or go online to find a complete list of plural noun forms.

- Some nouns refer to groups of people, but they have a singular form. In this case, they are called *collective nouns*.

  EXAMPLE

  the jury, the faculty, the team

- Nouns often have *articles* in front of them. An article is a type of adjective. The article *a* (*an* in front of a vowel) is used with a non-specific noun and is called indefinite. The article *the* is used with a specific noun and is called definite. A table for the use of these articles follows.

	Singular	Plural
Indefinite	a, an	—
Definite	the	the

EXAMPLES

> I saw *a* beautiful tree this morning.
> I saw beautiful trees this morning.
> *The* tree I described to you is a maple.
> *The* trees that I described are maples.

- Other types of words are often placed in front of nouns. They indicate possession and are called possessive adjectives.

EXAMPLES

my car; *her* coat; *their* books

- Nouns occupy strategic positions in a sentence. Without nouns, a sentence would be meaningless.
- In a sentence, a noun has special relationships with the verb or verbs. One relationship is called *subject*. The other is called *object*.
    1. The *subjects* and *objects* of verbs are always nouns (or words used as nouns) or pronouns.
    2. The word *subject* means that the noun or pronoun tells who or what is involved in what the verb describes. In other words, the *subject* indicates who or what is *doing* something or *being* something.

EXAMPLES

The child ran across the street.
> The verb is the action verb *ran* (to run).
> The subject is the noun *child*.

We will go directly home after the concert.
> The verb is the action verb *will go* (to go).
> The subject is the personal pronoun *we*.

The rose garden is beautiful.
> The verb is the state of being/linking verb *is* (to be).
> The subject is the noun *garden* (The noun *rose* is used as an adjective that adds detail to the noun *garden*).

3. The word *object* means that the noun or pronoun describes the result of the action (*direct object*) or is receiving what the verb describes (*indirect object*).

EXAMPLE

The track students ran a mile.
Who is running? The students are involved in running; they are the ones *doing* the action of running; therefore, the noun *students* is the subject of the verb *ran*.
The students are running *what*? The noun *mile* describes what the students are running. It is the *direct object* of the verb *ran*.

EXAMPLE

I *gave an apple to the child.*
1. Who is involved in giving? I. This is the subject of *gave.*
2. I gave what? An *apple.* This is the direct object of *gave.*
3. I gave an apple to whom? *The child.* This is the indirect object of *gave.*

The indirect object is easy to recognize because of the preposition in front of it. However, if I say the same thing without the preposition, the word *child* is still the indirect object as in I *gave the child an apple.*

- Some nouns have similar endings. These endings help readers recognize nouns in a sentence. The types of endings are:
  -al
  -ance
  -ar
  -ence
  -er
  -ism
  -ist
  -ity
  -ment
  -ness
  -or
  -ship
  -sion
  -tion

EXAMPLES

nationalism, stance, immersion, relationship, sequence, harness, mentor, shipment, diversity, information, soloist, builder, maintenance, mortar, and arsenal

When you see the endings, you know that the word is a noun.

THE PRONOUN

Pronouns, by definition, replace nouns. They are sometimes used in place of nouns to avoid too much noun repetition and create a lighter and more pleasant style. Several types of pronouns exist, and they are used for different purposes.

Personal Pronouns

Personal pronouns represent persons and things in the singular and the plural for number, and in the feminine (she), masculine (he), and neutral (it) for gender. In a sentence, they take on different functions in relationship to the verb or verbs as nouns do. The following table shows these categories.

Persons	Subjective	Objective	Possessive		Reflexive
			Adjective	Pronoun	
first sing.	I	me	my	mine	myself
second sing.	you	you	your	yours	yourself
third sing.	she	her	her	hers	herself
	he	him	his	his	himself
	it	it	its		itself
first plural	we	us	our	ours	ourselves
second plural	you	you	your	yours	yourselves
third plural	they	them	their	theirs	themselves

In this table, the word *subjective* means that in a sentence, the pronoun in that category is the *subject of the verb*. The word *objective* means that, in that category, the pronoun is the *object of the verb* in the sentence. The word *possessive* means that, in that category, the pronoun in the sentence indicates ownership. The word *reflexive* means that the pronoun in that category reflects back to the person with the ending *-self* for emphasis.

In the *possessive* category, there are both adjectives and pronouns. The *possessive adjectives* are used with nouns (*her* dress) and the *possessive pronouns* are used by themselves (this dress is *hers*).

Reflexive Pronouns

These pronouns have already been listed in the previous personal pronoun table. They add the ending *-self* to some personal pronouns for personal emphasis.

> **EXAMPLE**
>
> myself, yourself, yourselves, himself, herself, itself, ourselves, themselves

Possessive Pronouns

As listed in the previous table, these pronouns indicate possession or ownership.

Note that they are never written with an apostrophe. Pay special attention to the possessive *its*, which is never spelled with an apostrophe. When spelled with an apostrophe (*it's*), it is the contraction of *it is* (neutral personal pronoun subject third person singular with the verb *to be* in the third person present tense).

Demonstrative Pronouns

These pronouns are used to point or draw attention to things and people in the singular and the plural. They also distinguish between pointing to something or someone close and pointing further away.

Singular	Plural	
this	these	**CLOSE**
that	those	**FURTHER AWAY**

EXAMPLES

What kinds of fruits are *these* over here?
What kinds of fruits are *those* over there?
This is the place, right here.
That, over there, is her office.

Interrogative Pronouns

These are used to ask questions. The interrogative pronouns are: *who, whom, whose, which, what.*

EXAMPLES

Who is at the door?
With *whom* are you going to the movies?
Whose books are these?
Which seat would you like?
What time is it?

Relative Pronouns

The relative pronouns are the same as the interrogative pronouns. In addition, they include the words *that, whoever, whomever, whichever, whatever.*

When speaking of *persons*, use WHO.
When speaking of *things*, use WHICH.
Use THAT for either things or persons, preferably for things only.

EXAMPLES

1. This is the student *who* is going to give the commencement address.
2. The girl *who* is standing on the sidewalk is soaking wet.
3. Jim's uncle, *who* is a physicist, will be going on the lecture circuit this year.
4. The president, *whom* we elected, is doing a good job.
5. The young man to *whom* this car belongs cannot be found.
6. The person *whose* car is illegally parked will get a ticket.
7. All fallen debris *which* obstruct the highway will be removed.
8. The complete speech, *which* was very long, was recorded on tape.
9. The moments *that* we love are those we spend at home together.
10. No one knew *that* the elections would take such a turn.

Indefinite Pronouns

The indefinite pronouns refer to persons and things in a vague way. Some are always singular, some are always plural, and some can be either singular or plural. Below is a list of indefinite pronouns.

- **Always singular**—another, anybody, anyone, anything, each, either, everybody, everyone, everything, neither, nobody, no one, nothing, one, somebody, someone, something
- **Always plural**—both, few, many, others, several
- **Singular or plural**—all, any, more, most, none, some, such (they are used like collective nouns, either in the singular or the plural)

THE ADJECTIVE

The definition of an adjective makes it easy to recognize in a sentence. All words that add detail to nouns and pronouns are adjectives. Sometimes nouns are used in the function of an adjective.

- They are usually placed directly next to the noun or pronoun that they describe.

  EXAMPLE

  The wonderful blue sky enchanted me.
  In this sentence, *wonderful* and *blue* are adjectives that add detail to the noun *sky*.

- A unique way to use adjectives is after a linking verb. In this case, the adjective adds to the noun even when it is placed after the linking verb instead of directly next to the noun.

  EXAMPLE

  He was not feeling anxious before the test.
  In this example, the adjective *anxious* describes the pronoun *he* but is placed after the linking verb *was feeling*.

- Adjectives are useful to indicate the degree of what they describe. The adjective *strong* can be used in the degree of *stronger* or *strongest*.

  EXAMPLES

  1. She is *strong*.
  2. She is *stronger than* her brother. (comparison between two items)
  3. She is *the strongest of* all her siblings. (comparisons with all items)

- When the adjective is a long word, however, this is done by adding the words *more* and *most*.

  EXAMPLES

  1. This story is *more touching than* the one we read yesterday.
  2. His music is *the most beautiful* thing I ever heard.

THE ADVERB

The adverb does for the verb what the adjective does for the noun. Adverbs add details to verbs, but they are also used to add details to adjectives and other adverbs.

EXAMPLES
1. I did badly on the test. (*badly* adds detail to the verb *did*)
2. The pie is very good. (*very* adds detail to the adjective *good*)
3. They ran very fast. (*very* adds detail to the adverb *fast*)

Adverbs take many forms.

- Some of them are created from adjectives.

  EXAMPLE

  beautiful (adjective); beautifully (adverb)

- Others have irregular forms.

  EXAMPLES

  good (adjective); well (adverb)

- The word *not*, which is often used to indicate the negative, is an adverb.

THE VERB

No sentence exists without at least one verb in it. It is the heart of the sentence, and all meaning evolves from it. A group of words without at least one verb in it cannot be called a sentence. Many things need to be learned about verbs. A list of these follows.

- Four types of verbs exist: *action* verbs, *state of being* verbs (also known as *linking*), verbs that can be used either as action or as linking verbs, and *auxiliaries* (also known as *helping*).
  1. *Action verb*: This verb is about DOING.

  EXAMPLES

  to run, to like, to work, to think

  2. *Linking or state of being verb*: This verb is about BEING.

  EXAMPLES

  to be, to become, to seem

  3. Verbs that can be both *action* and *state of being*.

  EXAMPLES

  to appear, to feel, to grow, to look, to prove, to remain, to smell, to sound, to taste, to turn

  4. *Auxiliary or helping verbs*: These verbs help create various tenses, questions, and negatives.

EXAMPLES

1. The party must have been enjoyable for you to stay so long.
   In this example, *must* is an auxiliary; *have* is an auxiliary; *been* is the main verb in the past participle form.
2. Did you lock the doors?
   In this example, *did* is an auxiliary; *lock* is the main verb.
3. They do not eat big meals at night.
   In this example, *do* is the auxiliary; *eat* is the main verb.

- All verbs belong to two categories: *regular* and *irregular*.
  1. *Regular verbs*: They use a standard form in the past tense, *-ed* or *-d* ending.

EXAMPLES

They like the music. I *liked* the concert last night.
We study at the library. Last night, we *studied* for three hours.

  2. *Irregular verbs*: They are called irregular because their past tense takes many different forms. These must be memorized for the irregular verbs that are used most often. A list of most irregular verbs should be kept handy as a reference for all others.

EXAMPLES

To eat: I *ate* too much last night. The whole pie *was eaten* in ten minutes.
To run: He *ran* for thirty minutes. You *have run* out of time.

- All verbs are divided into three groups: *transitive*, *intransitive*, and verbs that can be both.
  1. A *transitive verb* does not make sense without an object.

EXAMPLE

The voters elected.
The verb *elected* alone does not carry a full meaning. An *object* is necessary to complete the sentence. For instance,

The voters elected the most charismatic candidate.
Now, the sentence makes sense. The verb *to elect* is a *transitive verb*.

  2. An *intransitive verb* cannot take an object.

EXAMPLE

They acted *without thinking*.
There is no object to the verb *acted*. The words *without thinking* are not a direct object. You cannot ask the question "They acted what?" and answer it with the words *without thinking*. These words answer the question: They acted *how*?

  3. Some verbs can be used either as *transitive* or *intransitive verbs*.

EXAMPLE

The verb to leave.
  Transitive: I will *leave you* to do your homework in peace. (*You* is the direct object of *leave*.)
  Intransitive: We are already late. We must *leave*. (There is no direct object.)

- Verbs are used in different forms called *tenses* to refer to different times.
  Verb tenses can become very complicated. They require that you understand the variations in meaning along the time continuum from past to future. See the Templates in Chapter 2 for verb tenses.
- Four verb forms must be known in order to create many others: the *infinitive*, the *present tense*, the *simple past tense*, and the *past participle*. See the Templates in Chapter 2 for an understanding of their use.
- Verbs are used in an *active voice*, a *passive voice*, or a *progressive voice*.

> **EXAMPLES**
>
> 1. Active voice: Jose *did* not *learn* to swim until he was fifteen.
> 2. Passive voice: My parents *were attracted* by a better life in America.
>   This sentence in the active form becomes:
>   > A *better life attracted my parents to America.*
> 3. Progressive voice: The accountants *are conducting* an audit of our firm.
>   The progressive voice indicates that the action is currently taking place.

- Some words are derived from verbs but are not verbs. These *verbals* are: the *infinitive*, the *gerund* (used as a noun), and the *participle, past or present* (used as adjectives).

It is imperative to NOT CONFUSE *verbals* with *verbs*.

1. The *infinitive* is the basic form of a verb with the preposition *to* in front of it. It is used simply to refer to a specific verb outside of a sentence.

> **EXAMPLE**
>
> *to earn, to study, to play*

2. The *gerund* has an *-ing* ending. It is often used as a noun, either as the subject or object in the sentence.

> **EXAMPLE**
>
> Running *is good for you.*
> *Running* is not a verb. It is a verbal called the *gerund*. It is the subject of the verb *is*. The only verb in the sentence is the word *is*.

3. The *present participle* also has an *-ing* ending, but it is usually used as an adjective.

> **EXAMPLE**
>
> The unending *complaints irritated him.*
> *Unending* is an adjective that adds detail to the noun *complaints*.

4. The *past participle* takes the ending *-ed* or *-d* with regular verbs and has various forms in irregular verbs. It is often used as an adjective.

> **EXAMPLE**
>
> Confused *by the oncoming headlights, the deer froze in the middle of the road.*
> *Confused* is an adjective that adds detail to the noun *deer*.

Here is another sentence:

> **EXAMPLE**
>
> The *situation* could have become alarming.
> In this sentence, *become* is not a verb; it is a verbal called *past participle* but it is included in the verb.
> The verb is three words: the verbal *become* and the auxiliaries *could have*.

- In a sentence, a verb must have a subject and a tense. A transitive verb must also have a direct object.
- As a result of the special relationship between the verb and its subject, special rules exist for them. They are referred to as *subject-verb agreement* rules. When a subject is singular, the verb must also be in a singular form. When the subject is plural, the verb must take a plural form. A singular subject is any noun in the singular and pronouns in the first, second, or third person singular. A plural subject is any plural noun or any plural pronoun, first, second, or third person plural.

In order to know whether a verb is in the singular or the plural form, learn the following rule:

> The only change in a verb form is in the present tense, third person singular: an *-s* is added.

> **EXAMPLES**
>
> 1. The food *spoils* when kept outside of the refrigerator. (*Food* is a singular subject, third person; an *-s* is added to the verb *spoil* so subject and verb agree.)
> 2. The trees show the signs of autumn.
> 3. The maple tree *shows* the signs of autumn. (*Tree* is a third person singular subject; an *-s* is added to the verb *show* so verb and subject agree.)
> 4. We like to hike in the mountains.
> 5. She *likes* to shop for Christmas. (*She* is a third person singular subject; an *-s* is added to the verb *like* so subject and verb agree.)

Be sure to remember that this *-s* is not a plural.

THE PREPOSITION

Prepositions are used to join words and groups of words to indicate a connection with another part of the sentence. A preposition acquires a specific meaning when added to other words.

> **EXAMPLES**
>
> 1. I sat *on* the bench.
> 2. We snacked *before* lunch.
> 3. The picture was taken *in front of* the White House.

THE CONJUNCTION

Conjunctions also connect words and groups of words. There are two types:

1. *The coordinating conjunction* can be used to connect two words or two clauses, both independent.
2. *The subordinating conjunction* is used to connect one independent clause with a dependent one. The subordinating conjunction opens the dependent clause.

Conjunctions have strict rules of punctuation attached to them.

THE INTERJECTION

Interjections do not have special relationships with other words in the sentence as nouns, pronouns, and verbs do. Their function is to express various emotions like surprise, anger, relief, and others. They are sometimes followed by an exclamation mark (!).

EXAMPLES

oh, well, wow

2

GRAMMATICAL REFERENCE TEMPLATES

The templates serve as handy quick reference tools that summarize the information given in Chapter 1.

TEMPLATE 1—FROM WORDS TO SENTENCES

WORDS

PHRASES

CLAUSES

SENTENCES

- A few words *without a verb* are a PHRASE.
- A few words *with at least one verb* are a CLAUSE.
    - A clause that makes complete sense is **independent.**
    - A clause that requires more words for full meaning is **dependent.**
- A few words *with at least one verb and complete meaning* are a SENTENCE.
    - An independent clause is the same as a sentence since a sentence is defined as a group of words that includes at least one verb and makes complete sense.
- A sentence starts with a capital letter on the first word and ends with a period.

TEMPLATE 2—PHRASES

Definition: a group of words without a verb

Types

- Prepositional:

  EXAMPLE

  In the morning, she usually eats a large breakfast.
  > *In* is a preposition.
  > *In the morning* is a prepositional phrase.

- Infinitive:

  EXAMPLE

  Jamie and Jill offer to help.
  To help is an infinitive (the basic form of the verb with the preposition *to* in front of it).

- Participial:

  EXAMPLE

  Children watching a lot of television do not do well at school.
  > *Watching* is a present participle.
  > *Watching* is used as an adjective for *children*.
  > *Watching a lot of television* is a participial phrase.

  Born in a family of twelve, I learned early the value of sharing.
  > *Born* is a past participle.
  > *Born* is an adjective for I.
  > *Born in a family of twelve* is a participial phrase.

- Gerund:

  EXAMPLE

  Going on fad diets deceives many about their weight problems.
  > *Going* is a gerund used as the subject of the verb *deceives*.
  > *Going on fad diets* is the subject of the verb *deceives*.
  > *Going on fad diets* is a gerund phrase.

- Absolute:

  EXAMPLE

  Her vacation almost finished, she resolutely began to think about her studies.
  The sweat covering his brow, he tried to regain his composure.
  > The absolute phrase is not grammatically related to the rest of the sentence.

TEMPLATE 3—CLAUSES

Definition: a group of words with at least one verb

Types

- *Dependent*: It contains a subject and a verb, but it does not make a complete thought. It depends on another group of words to acquire complete meaning.

  EXAMPLES

  > As soon as you finish your homework . . .
  > Before she had a chance to finish her sentence . . .
  > . . . who was standing on the sidewalk . . .
  > . . . that we loved so much . . .
  > What he said . . .

  If a period is used at the end of these clauses, a fragment is created.
  Fragments are serious writing errors.

- *Independent*: It contains at least one verb and its subject, and it makes a complete thought.

  Since this is also the definition of a sentence, an independent clause is also a sentence.

  EXAMPLES

  > *The new freeway has relieved traffic congestion.* (one independent clause)
  > *On weekends, we usually relax and play with our children.* (one independent clause)
  > *Her brothers enjoyed playing with her, but she often thought they were too rough.* (two independent clauses joined by *and*)

TEMPLATE 4—SENTENCES

Definition: A group of words that include at least one verb and its subject and make complete sense.

Types

- *Simple*: It is made of one independent clause.

    EXAMPLES

    He is anxious.
    She bought a complete winter wardrobe at Macy's.
    That house is too small for our family.
    After school, she immediately went to her room to study.

- *Compound*: It is made of two or more independent clauses connected with a conjunction of coordination.

    EXAMPLES

    Steve plays drums, but he never takes time to practice.
    Jess enjoys school, yet he struggles with some subjects.
    They drove up the hill, and they set out the picnic in a shady spot.

- *Complex*: It is made of one independent clause and one or more dependent clauses connected with conjunctions of subordinations, relative pronouns, or conjunctive adverbs.

    EXAMPLES

    You can play with me as soon as you finish your homework.
    While I stood there, dazed, the building collapsed.
    Whenever I want to take a nap, my dog wants to go for a walk.
    The nurse who took care of me has a nice bedside manner.
    The photographs that you developed are all ruined.
    Gasoline, which smells bad, should not be inhaled.

- *Compound/Complex*: This is one sentence that combines the compound and complex structures.

    EXAMPLE

    As I walked slowly into the forest, the air became cooler, and the day became dusk.

TEMPLATE 5—PUNCTUATION

Definition: The use of symbols such as the comma (,), the semicolon (;), the period (.), the colon (:), the exclamation mark (!), and the question mark (?).

The comma and the period are the most commonly used punctuation marks. Incorrect use of punctuation creates three serious errors in writing: the *fragment*, the *comma splice*, and the *run-on*. Knowledge of the definition of phrases, clauses, and sentences is vital in order to punctuate sentences correctly. See Templates 1 through 4.

- Only the period and the semicolon are strong enough to separate independent clauses. The difference between them is that, after a period, you must capitalize the first word of the next sentence.

- The *comma* is too weak to separate independent clauses. You can use it in that situation only when followed by a conjunction of coordination, creating a compound sentence.

TEMPLATE 6—THE COMMA

The comma is the most frequently used punctuation mark. It is used in the following situations:

- To separate two independent clauses within the same sentence ONLY IF followed by a coordinating conjunction. However, use no comma if the subject is the same in both clauses *and is* not repeated in the second clause as in this sentence.

- After a prepositional phrase that introduces a sentence.

  EXAMPLE

  After her swim, she went to her room to study.

- After any kind of introductory phrase.

  EXAMPLE

  Forever grateful, the family wrote a long letter of thanks.

- Between every item in dates and places.

  EXAMPLE

  He was born on January 12, 1887, in Atlanta, Georgia.

- Between items in a series.

  EXAMPLE

  Here are pens, pencils, markers, paper, and erasers.

- On each side of any word or phrase that interrupts the main thought.

  EXAMPLE

  No one, least of all the students, objected to the change in plans.

- With contrasted elements.

  EXAMPLE

  Go up, not down.

TEMPLATE 7—THE POSSESSIVE CASE

The possessive case indicates the idea of belonging, ownership, or possession. In order to write the possessive case correctly, one must understand the *difference between the possessive case and the plural of nouns*.

Most nouns take -*s* when put in the plural. But a few nouns are irregular in their plural forms.

EXAMPLES

one tree   four trees
one child   four children

The possessive case is written in two different ways, one for a singular noun and the other for a plural noun or an irregular plural. The punctuation mark called *apostrophe* is used.

EXAMPLES

the tree**'s** leaves   the trees' leaves
the child**'s** lunch   the children's lunch

Important Note: When using the apostrophe, remember that a letter space is needed for it. Never eliminate the apostrophe or the space.

TEMPLATE 8—VERB TENSES

- Verbs/Regular

EXAMPLE

to like

- Active Voice
- Present Tense
  Action occurs in the present.

EXAMPLES	SINGULAR	PLURAL
First person	I like	we like
Second person	you like	you like
Third person	he, she, it like<u>s</u>	they like

- Past Tense
  Action occurred in the past.

EXAMPLES	SINGULAR	PLURAL
First person	I liked	we liked
Second person	you liked	you liked
Third person	he, she, it liked	they liked

- Future Tense
  Action will occur in the future.

EXAMPLES	SINGULAR	PLURAL
First person	I will/shall like	we will like
Second person	you will like	you will like
Third person	he, she, it will like	they will like

- Present Perfect Tense
  Action began in the past and still occurs.

EXAMPLES	SINGULAR	PLURAL
First person	I have like<u>d</u>	we have liked
Second person	you have liked	you have liked
Third person	he, she, it <u>has</u> liked	they have liked

- Past Perfect Tense
  Action started and completed in the past.

EXAMPLES	SINGULAR	PLURAL
First person	I had liked	we had liked
Second person	you had liked	you had liked
Third person	he, she, it had liked	they had liked

- Future Perfect Tense
Action will be completed in the future.

EXAMPLES	SINGULAR	PLURAL
First person	I will have like	we will have liked
Second person	you will have liked	you will have liked
Third person	he will have liked	they will have liked

- Passive Voice

EXAMPLES

I am liked.
I was liked.
I will be liked.
I have been liked.
I had been liked.
I will have been liked.

- Progressive Form
Action currently occurring.
This form can be used in all the tenses.

ACTIVE	PASSIVE
I am liking	I am being liked
I was liking	I was being liked
I will be liking	
I have been liking	
I had been liking	
I will have been liking	

- Participles

EXAMPLES

Active Present: liking
Active Past: liked
Active Perfect: having liked
Passive Present: being liked
Passive Past: been liked
Passive Perfect: having been liked

Note: All regular verbs end in *-ed* in the past tense and the past participle.

- Verbs/Irregular
Verbs are called irregular when they have different forms within their own conjugation. These verbs must be memorized in the following forms: *Present tense, past tense, past participle,* and *present participle.*
Knowing these forms will allow you to use the verbs in all tense combinations.

TEMPLATE 9—LINKING VERBS

These verbs are also named *state of being* verbs because they do not express action. They describe a state of being.

Some verbs are true linking verbs because they are always linking verbs. They often refer to the five senses and they link the subject to information about the subject. For that reason, they are intransitive. Others can be used as linking or as action verbs.

True Linking Verbs

EXAMPLES	
To be	*My father is a businessman.*
To become	*We become tired quickly.*
To appear	*She appears troubled.*
To seem	*You seem apprehensive.*
To look	*Paul looks happy.*
To go	*She goes crazy.*
To remain	*My grandfather remains active.*

Hybrid Verbs, Linking or Action

EXAMPLES	
To feel	*I feel dizzy. She feels the soft fabric.*
To grow	*They grew wild. She grows a new type of strawberry.*
To sound	*The principal sounds harsh. They sounded the alarm.*
To smell	*The milk smells sour. He smells the delicate aroma.*
To turn	*His face turned green. They turned the page quickly.*
To taste	*This food tastes rotten. We taste a new dish.*
To run	*The kids ran wild. You run a mile each day.*
To get	*Don't get serious. I will get good grades.*

The examples show that linking verbs are often followed by adjectives. When used as action verbs, they take objects.

TEMPLATE 10—TRANSITIVE AND INTRANSITIVE VERBS

- Transitive verbs are used with direct objects. They answer the question WHAT.

  EXAMPLE

  I *love this music.*
  I love WHAT? This music.

- Intransitive verbs are not followed by direct objects and would not make sense if they did. They answer the questions HOW, WHERE, WHEN, and WHY.

  EXAMPLE

  The old woman struggles across the street.

- Verbs can be both transitive and intransitive.

  EXAMPLES

  Intransitive: *Her grandfather moves slowly.*
  Transitive: *They moved all the furniture in one hour.*

TEMPLATE 11—COORDINATING CONJUNCTIONS

Meaning	Conjunction
Addition	and
Contrast	but, yet
Consequence	so
Alternative	or, nor
Cause	for

The conjunction *nor* is used in a special way. It follows a negative statement and requires changing the order of the verb and subject.

EXAMPLE

Laura did not look for a job, nor did she expect to find one.

The use of commas with conjunctions of coordination is described in the Comma template.

Another type of conjunction will be listed here. It always appears in pairs of words. One word in the pair is a conjunction of coordination.

EXAMPLE

Both . . . and
Either . . . or
Neither . . . nor
Not only . . . but also
So . . . as
Whether . . . or

No comma is used with these.

EXAMPLE

Both my father and mother died when I was young.

TEMPLATE 12—SUBORDINATING CONJUNCTIONS

Meaning	Conjunction
Time	after, before, when, whenever, while, as, as long as, until, as soon as, since, once
Place	where, wherever
Purpose	so that, as, because, since, in order that
Condition	if, as if, unless, when, whether, even if, if only, provided
Contrast	although, even though, though, while, whereas, rather than
Cause/effect	because, since, so that, now that

The rules for comma use with subordinating conjunctions are:

- When the conjunction starts the sentence, a comma is needed before the independent clause starts.

  EXAMPLE

  When I study, I don't hear anything.

- When the conjunction does not start the sentence, no comma is used.

  EXAMPLE

  I don't hear anything when I study.

TEMPLATE 13—RELATIVE PRONOUNS

> who, whom, whose, which, that
> whoever, whomever, whichever

- Use WHO, WHOEVER, WHOM, WHOMEVER, WHOSE when speaking about PEOPLE.

- Use WHICH and WHICHEVER when speaking about THINGS or IDEAS.

- Use THAT when speaking about either but preferably about THINGS or IDEAS.

TEMPLATE 14—CONJUNCTIVE ADVERBS

Meaning	Conjunctive Adverb
Addition	also, further, furthermore, in addition, moreover, besides
Contrast	however, instead, nevertheless, otherwise, on the other hand
Time	meanwhile, then, afterwards, next, now, later
Result	as a result, consequently, therefore
Reality	in fact, indeed, that is, thus, in other words, for example

The punctuation rules for conjunctive adverbs are:

- Semicolon in front of it and comma after it.

  EXAMPLE

  He was mad; however, it did not last.

- Period in front of it and comma after it.

  EXAMPLE:

  He was mad. However, it did not last.

- A comma on each side of it.

  EXAMPLE

  The wind was blowing hard. The air, however, was not cold.

TEMPLATE 15—PREPOSITIONS

about, above, across, after, against, along, among, around, at,

before, behind, below, beneath, beside, between, beyond, by,

despite, during,

except,

for, from,

in, inside, into,

like,

near,

of, off, on, onto, out, outside, over,

through, throughout, to, toward,

under, underneath, until, up, upon,

with, within, without

Prepositions are always used with nouns and pronouns only. Adjectives can be added to the nouns. These words together become a prepositional phrase as in the following: *After a scrumptious lunch.*

If some of these words are used with verbs following them, they are no longer prepositions. They are conjunctions as in the following: *After they had finished their lunch.*

TEMPLATE 16—PERSONAL PRONOUNS AND ADJECTIVES

Persons	Subjective	Objective	Possessive		Reflexive
			Adjective	Pronoun	
first sing.	I	me	my	mine	myself
second sing.	you	you	your	yours	yourself
third sing.	she	her	her	hers	herself
	he	him	his	his	himself
	it	it	its		itself
first plural	we	us	our	ours	ourselves
second plural	you	you	your	yours	yourselves
third plural	they	them	their	theirs	themselves

TEMPLATE 17—INDEFINITE PRONOUNS

Always Singular

another, anybody, anyone, anything, each, either, everybody, everyone, everything, neither, nobody, no one, nothing, one, somebody, someone, something

Always Plural

both, few, many, others, several

Singular or Plural

all, any, more, most, none, some, such (*they are used like collective nouns, either in the singular or the plural*).

TEMPLATE 18—COMMA SPLICES

The comma splice occurs when two independent clauses are separated by a comma without a co-ordinating conjunction.

EXAMPLE OF A COMMA SPLICE

They drove up the hill, they set out the picnic in a shady spot.

Correction
They drove up the hill, and they set out the picnic in a shady spot.

EXAMPLE OF A COMMA SPLICE

Jamie likes school, she struggles in math.

Correction
Jamie likes school, but she struggles in math.

TEMPLATE 19—RUN-ONS

The run-on sentence is created in the following situations:

- Two or more independent clauses are not separated by anything.

  They drove up the hill they set out the picnic in a shady spot.

  Correction
  They drove up the hill, and they set out the picnic in a shady spot.

- Two independent clauses are separated by a coordinating conjunction without a comma.

  They drove up the hill and they set out the picnic in a shady spot.

  Correction
  They drove up the hill, and they set out the picnic in a shady spot.

TEMPLATE 20—FRAGMENTS

A fragment is an incomplete sentence because it does not make complete sense even if it includes a verb.

- A phrase becomes a fragment if it ends with a period.

  EXAMPLE

  On weekends. We usually relax.

  Correction
  On weekends, we usually relax.

- A dependent clause becomes a fragment if it ends with a period.

  EXAMPLE

  As long as you are going out. Pick up some bread at the store.

  Correction
  As long as you are going out, pick up some bread at the store.

- Phrases and dependent clauses together make a fragment if they end with a period.

  EXAMPLE

  Without directions because they had lost their map. The hikers could not find the trail.

  Correction
  Without directions because they had lost their map, the hikers could not find the trail.

3

SENTENCE IMITATION: UNDERSTANDING STRUCTURE AND DEVELOPING VOCABULARY

In this chapter, you will imitate sentence structures. To do this correctly, you must first copy the model without errors, underline it, and write your sentence or sentences below it. You must choose the content of your sentence. In other words, you must tell a story that is different from the model, which requires that you change the words. You must, however, retain the structure of the sentence, which is based on the parts of speech studied in Chapter 2.

In order to find new words for your imitation, you may want to use the dictionary and even a thesaurus. The exercise will not only teach you the sentence structure but will also enrich your vocabulary.

Occasionally, one or two words from the model must be kept in the imitation because you are learning to use that specific word. When this is the case, it is clearly indicated at the beginning of that workshop, and the words to be retained are underlined in the model. Otherwise, you must change all the words.

Conscious and thoughtful imitation is key to successful learning outcomes, and repetition ensures memorization and integration of the material. As soon as you are able to imitate certain sentences a dozen times without mistakes, you should move to other workshops where you can practice with more complex sentence construction. Eventually, you will learn to create your own combinations of several structures into a single sentence. When you reach this level successfully, you demonstrate competency in controlling writing options the language offers.

In the first workshop, Workshop A, each sentence structure is identified and a detailed diagram of it is given to help you review the parts of speech. You must get in the habit of identifying the words in a sentence before imitating it. This makes Workshop A fairly difficult because every word in the model must be replaced exactly by the same type of word in your imitation. You will go slowly through this workshop, doing only two or three sentences at a time. What matters is to learn the process and practice it accurately. A sample imitation is given for each sentence to show you how correct imitation is done. Workshop A emphasizes identification of verbs and their subjects.

In subsequent workshops, the sentence structure is not diagrammed, but you must do it in your head to ensure that your imitation is correct. After Workshop A, you are no longer required to imitate every single word as in the model, but you must maintain the integrity of the sentence by keeping the underlined words and reproducing the punctuation required with that structure. After Workshop B, imitation examples are given only occasionally.

WORKSHOP A—SIMPLE SENTENCES WITH TRANSITIVE ACTION VERBS

Simple sentences are constructed with one independent clause. They must have at least one *verb* and its *subject*. However, they can have one *verb* with several *subjects*, one *subject* with several *verbs*, or several *subjects* with several *verbs*. You can have a simple sentence with an *object* in addition to the *subject* and *verb* only when the *verb* is *transitive*. In this workshop, you will imitate simple sentences that include *objects* to an *action verb*. Both *regular action verbs* and *irregular action verbs* will be used.

In this workshop, change all the words except the ones that are underlined. Keep the sentence structure.

- Simple sentence with one noun subject to one regular verb in the present tense.

1. **Model:** <u>A</u> plastic sheet covers <u>the</u> precious photographs.

   Structure: indefinite article + noun used as adjective + noun subject + verb (regular, transitive, present tense, third person singular) + definite article + adjective + noun object

   Imitation: An arbitrary decision concludes the difficult negotiations.

   Your imitation:

   _____

   _____

- Simple sentence with one noun subject to one irregular verb in the present tense.
2. **Model:** <u>My</u> elderly uncle grows gorgeous roses.

   Structure: possessive adjective, first person singular + adjective + noun subject + verb (irregular, transitive, present tense, third person singular) + adjective + noun object

   Imitation: My old shirt makes excellent rags.

   Your Imitation:

   _____

   _____

- Simple sentence with one personal pronoun in the third person singular subject to one regular verb in the present tense.
3. **Model:** <u>He</u> carefully finishes <u>the</u> last chapter.

   Structure: personal pronoun subject, third personal singular, male gender + adverb + verb (regular, transitive, present tense, third person singular) + definite article + adjective + noun object

   Imitation: He abruptly ends the tense conversation.

   Your Imitation:

   _____

   _____

- Simple sentence with one personal pronoun in the third person singular subject to one irregular verb in the present tense.

4. **Model:** <u>She</u> conscientiously writes <u>a</u> detailed journal entry.

   Structure: personal pronoun subject, third person singular, female gender + adverb + verb (irregular, transitive, present tense, third person singular) + indefinite article + adjective + noun used as adjective + noun object

   Imitation: She accidentally breaks a beautiful glass figurine.

   Your imitation:

   _____

   _____

- Simple sentence with one personal pronoun subject to one regular verb in the present tense.

5. **Model:** <u>They</u> love <u>the</u> new principal.

   Structure: personal pronoun subject, third person plural + verb (regular, transitive, present tense, third person plural) + definite article + adjective + noun object

   Imitation: They prepare the special meal.

   Your Imitation:

   _____

   _____

- Simple sentence with one personal pronoun subject to one irregular verb in the present tense.

6. **Model:** <u>We</u> buy <u>a</u> complete new wardrobe.

   Structure: personal pronoun subject, first person plural + verb (irregular, transitive, present tense, plural) + indefinite article + adjective + adjective + noun object

   Imitation: We catch a large squirmy fish.

   Your Imitation:

   _____

   _____

- Simple sentence with several nouns subjects to one regular verb in the present tense.

7. **Model:** <u>The</u> guide <u>and</u> <u>the</u> hikers study <u>the</u> map carefully.

   Structure: definite article + noun subject singular + coordinating conjunction + definite article + noun subject plural + verb (regular, transitive, present tense, plural) + definite article + noun object + adverb

   Imitation: The CEO and the managers prepare the meeting together.

   Your Imitation:

   _____

   _____

- Simple sentence with several noun subjects to one irregular verb in the present tense.
8. **Model:** Nancy, Matt, and Larry break the laughing record.

   Structure: noun subject + noun subject + coordination conjunction + noun subject + verb (irregular, transitive, present tense, plural) + definite article + adjective + noun object

   Imitation: The diary, the conversations, and the memories make an interesting novel.

   Your Imitation:

   _____

   _____

- Simple sentence with several personal pronoun subjects to one regular verb in the present tense.

9. **Model:** <u>She</u> <u>and</u> I study <u>our</u> complicated biology text.

   Structure: personal pronoun subject, third person singular + coordinating conjunction + personal pronoun subject, first person singular + verb (regular, transitive, present tense, plural) + possessive adjective, first person plural + adjective + noun used as adjective + noun object

   Imitation: She and I donate our precious stamp collection.

   Your Imitation:

   _____

   _____

- Simple sentence with several personal pronoun subjects to one irregular verb in the present tense.
10. **Model:** <u>You</u> <u>and</u> I sing <u>the</u> latest hits together.

    Structure: personal pronoun subject, second person singular or plural + coordinating conjunction + personal pronoun subject, first person singular + verb (irregular transitive, present tense, plural) + definite article + adjective + noun object + adverb

    Imitation: You and I undertake the delicate repairs skillfully.

    Your Imitation:

    _____

    _____

- Simple sentence with a gerund used as a noun subject to a regular verb in the present tense.
11. **Model:** Running promotes respiratory <u>and</u> muscular health.

    Structure: gerund used as noun subject + verb (regular, transitive, present tense, third person singular) + adjective + coordinating conjunction + adjective + noun object

    Imitation: Dreaming reveals personal and emotional conflicts.

    Your Imitation:

    _____

    _____

- Simple sentence with two gerunds used as nouns and as subjects to an irregular verb in the present tense.

12. **Model:** Proofreading <u>and</u> editing give quality output.

    Structure: gerund used as noun subject + coordinating conjunction + gerund used as noun subject + verb (irregular, transitive, present tense, third person plural) + noun used as adjective + noun object

    Imitation: Weeping and talking provide emotional relief.

    Your Imitation:

    _____

    _____

- Simple sentence with one noun subject to several regular verbs in the present tense.

13. **Model:** <u>The</u> young dancer studies <u>and</u> executes <u>the</u> new step.

    Structure: definite article + adjective + noun subject + verb (regular, transitive, present tense, third person singular) + coordinating conjunction + verb (regular, transitive, present tense, third person singular) + definite article + adjective + noun object

    Imitation: The subtle hint confuses and embarrasses the shy foreigner.

    Your Imitation:

    _____

    _____

- Simple sentence with one noun subject to several irregular verbs in the present tense.

14. **Model:** <u>My</u> dear nephew catches, feeds, <u>and</u> keeps stray cats.

    Structure: Personal possessive adjective + adjective + noun + verb (regular, transitive, present tense, third person singular) + verb (regular, transitive, present tense, third person singular) + coordinating conjunction + verb (regular, transitive, present tense, third person singular) + adjective + noun object

    Imitation: My old friend buys, rebuilds, and resells abandoned houses.

    Your Imitation:

    _____

    _____

- Simple sentence with one personal pronoun in the third person singular with several regular verbs in the present tense.

15. **Model:** <u>She</u> enjoys <u>and</u> plays <u>the</u> piano every day.

    Structure: Personal pronoun subject, feminine, third person singular + verb (regular, transitive, present tense, third person singular) + coordinating conjunction + verb (regular, transitive, present tense, third person singular) + definite article + noun object + adverb

Imitation: She bakes and decorates the cakes artistically.
Your Imitation:

_____

_____

- Simple sentence with one personal pronoun in the third personal singular with several irregular verbs in the present tense.
16. **Model:** <u>It</u> grows roots, spreads runners, <u>and</u> overtakes the small backyard.

    Structure: Personal pronoun, third person singular, neutral + verb (irregular, transitive, present tense, third person singular) + noun object + verb (irregular, transitive, present tense, third person singular) + noun object + coordinating conjunction + verb (irregular, transitive, present tense, third person singular) + definite article adjective + noun object

    Imitation: It stings humans, burns the skin, and spreads a deadly disease.

    Your Imitation:

    _____

    _____

- Simple sentence with one personal pronoun subject to several regular verbs in the present tense.
17. **Model:** <u>We</u> listen, study, <u>and</u> ask many questions.

    Structure: Personal pronoun subject, first person plural + verb (regular, transitive, present tense, first person plural) + verb (regular, transitive, present tense, first person plural) + coordinating conjunction + verb (regular, transitive, present tense, first person plural) + adjective + noun object

    Imitation: We sketch, color, and frame original watercolors.

    Your Imitation:

    _____

    _____

- Simple sentence with one personal pronoun subject to several irregular verbs in the present tense.
18. **Model:** <u>You</u> make <u>and</u> sell delicious cookies.

    Structure: Personal pronoun subject, second person singular + verb (irregular, transitive, present tense, second person singular) + coordinating conjunction + verb (irregular, transitive, present tense, second person singular) + adjective + noun object

    Imitation: You burn and hide music CDs.

    Your Imitation:

    _____

    _____

- Simple sentence with various subjects to regular verbs in the simple past tense.

19. **Model:** The parents and their children attended and enjoyed the puppet show.

    Structure: Indefinite article + noun subject + coordinating conjunction + personal pronoun possessive, third person plural + noun subject + verb (regular, transitive, simple past, third person plural) + coordinating conjunction + verb (regular, transitive, simple past, third person plural) + definite article + noun used as adjective + noun object

    Imitation: The singers and their musicians waited and boarded the crowded airplane.

    Your Imitation:

    _____

    _____

- Simple sentences with various subjects to irregular verbs in the simple past tense.

20. **Model:** The firefighters, the volunteers, and the homeowners gave their time and led the emergency efforts.

    Structure: Definite article + noun subject + definite article + noun subject + coordinating conjunction + definite article + noun subject + verb (irregular, transitive, third person plural, simple past) + personal pronoun possessive, third person plural + noun object + coordinating conjunction + verb (irregular, transitive, third person plural, simple past) + definite article + noun used as adjective + noun object

    Imitation: The cats, the dogs, and the rabbits fled their yard and made a miraculous escape.

    Your Imitation:

    _____

    _____

WORKSHOP B—SIMPLE SENTENCES WITH TRANSITIVE ACTION VERBS IN A VARIETY OF TENSES WITH AND WITHOUT AUXILIARIES

In this workshop, change all the words except the ones that are underlined. Keep the sentence structure.

1. **Model:** <u>The</u> girl bought <u>a</u> new dress.
   Sample Imitation: The child caught a bad cold.
   Your Imitations:

   _____

   _____

   _____

   _____

   _____

2. **Model:** Jamie slips <u>and</u> breaks <u>the</u> beautiful glass dish.
   Sample Imitation: Charlene peels and cuts the ripe green apple.
   Your Imitations:

   _____

   _____

3. **Model:** <u>They</u> finished <u>their</u> game late.
   Sample Imitation: They completed their homework early.
   Your Imitations:

   _____

   _____

   _____

4. **Model:** <u>A</u> beautiful linen covered <u>the</u> table.
   Sample Imitation: A pretty young girl jumped the hurdle.
   Your Imitations:

   _____

   _____

   _____

5. **Model:** <u>The</u> child badly scratched his knee yesterday.

   Sample Imitation: The pilot carefully landed the plane this morning.

   Your Imitations:

   _____

   _____

   _____

   _____

   _____

6. **Model:** Mrs. Thomas grew roses every year.

   Sample Imitation: My neighbor forgot his keys last night.

   Your Imitations:

   _____

   _____

   _____

   _____

   _____

7. **Model:** <u>The</u> soprano sang <u>a</u> beautiful song.

   Sample Imitation: The officer found a dead body.

   Your Imitations:

   _____

   _____

   _____

   _____

   _____

8. **Model:** <u>The</u> soprano sang <u>the</u> opera beautifully.

   Sample Imitation: The student gave the speech nervously.

   Your Imitations:

   _____

   _____

   _____

   _____

   _____

9. **Model:** <u>The</u> dean made <u>an</u> important announcement.
   Sample Imitation: The instructor gave an easy midterm.
   Your Imitations:

   _____

   _____

   _____

   _____

   _____

10. **Model:** <u>The</u> player made several mistakes.
    Sample Imitation: The coach gave precise instructions.
    Your Imitations:

    _____

    _____

    _____

    _____

    _____

11. **Model:** <u>The</u> experienced swimmers surfed high waves.
    Sample Imitation: The nasty rumors reached incredible proportions.
    Your Imitations:

    _____

    _____

    _____

    _____

    _____

12. **Model:** <u>My</u> father played several musical instruments.
    Sample Imitation: My business offered many useful services.
    Your Imitations:

    _____

    _____

    _____

    _____

    _____

13. **Model:** Bob always discovers interesting magazines.
    Sample Imitation: The bank often requires financial statements.
    Your Imitations:

    _____

    _____

    _____

    _____

    _____

14. **Model:** The spaniel fetched <u>the</u> stick.
    Sample Imitation: The surgeon removed the appendix.
    Your Imitations:

    _____

    _____

    _____

    _____

    _____

15. **Model:** Aaron paid his bills <u>this</u> morning.
    Sample Imitation: The lawyer pled the case this afternoon.
    Your Imitations:

    _____

    _____

    _____

    _____

16. **Model:** I just found <u>my</u> old tattered baseball cap.
    Sample Imitation: She suddenly tore my precious nursing class notes.
    Your Imitations:

    _____

    _____

    _____

    _____

    _____

17. **Model:** The science teacher asked <u>an</u> easy question.

    Sample Imitation: The apple trees provided an abundant crop.

    Your Imitations:

    _____

    _____

    _____

    _____

    _____

18. **Model:** You burned <u>the</u> same CD twice.

    Sample Imitation: She anxiously called the busy paramedics.

    Your Imitations:

    _____

    _____

    _____

    _____

    _____

19. **Model:** <u>She</u> bakes brownies <u>every</u> Sunday.

    Sample Imitation: She cleans the house every week.

    Your Imitations:

    _____

    _____

    _____

    _____

    _____

20. **Model:** <u>My</u> brother manages <u>the</u> new corner gas station.

    Sample Imitation: My textbook describes the best study skill methods.

    Your Imitations:

    _____

    _____

    _____

    _____

    _____

21. **Model:** <u>We</u> held <u>the</u> graduation exercises outside.
    Sample Imitation: We caught the masked robbers eventually.
    Your Imitations:

    _____

    _____

    _____

    _____

    _____

22. **Model:** <u>She</u> prefers hard candy.
    Sample Imitation: She arranges fancy cruises.
    Your Imitations:

    _____

    _____

    _____

    _____

    _____

23. **Model:** Amanda chose <u>the</u> red dress.
    Sample Imitation: The puppy tore the old slipper.
    Your Imitations:

    _____

    _____

    _____

    _____

    _____

24. **Model:** <u>My</u> friends wanted <u>an</u> elaborate party.
    Sample Imitation: My professors required a ten-page paper.
    Your Imitations:

    _____

    _____

    _____

    _____

    _____

25. **Model:** <u>She</u> revises all <u>her</u> papers.
    Sample Imitation: She invites her many friends.
    Your Imitations:

    _____

    _____

    _____

    _____

26. **Model:** <u>The</u> exhausted parents slowly sipped <u>their</u> tea.
    Sample Imitation: The precious stones clearly showed their brilliance.
    Your Imitations:

    _____

    _____

    _____

    _____

27. **Model:** <u>The</u> high winds broke <u>the</u> pretty umbrellas.
    Sample Imitation: The distraught teenager heard the bad news.
    Your Imitations:

    _____

    _____

    _____

    _____

28. **Model:** <u>The</u> librarian found me <u>the</u> books.
    Sample Imitation: The counselor taught me the strategies.
    Your Imitations:

    _____

    _____

    _____

    _____

29. **Model:** <u>Her</u> father sent <u>her</u> <u>some</u> college information.
    Sample Imitation: Her mistress threw her some raw meat.
    Your Imitations:

    _____

    _____

    _____

    _____

    _____

30. **Model:** <u>The</u> spaniel brought his master the long stick.
    Sample Imitation: The jury gave the defendant a second chance.
    Your Imitations:

    _____

    _____

    _____

    _____

    _____

31. **Model:** We sold <u>the</u> student <u>a</u> ticket.
    Sample Imitation: They fed the snake a mouse.
    Your Imitations:

    _____

    _____

    _____

    _____

    _____

32. **Model:** <u>The</u> attendant gave him a dirty look.
    Sample Imitation: The cashier handed me the wrong change.
    Your Imitations:

    _____

    _____

    _____

    _____

    _____

33. **Model:** They assign the young employee <u>the</u> toughest job.
    Sample Imitation: You offer the hungry kids the healthiest snacks.
    Your Imitations:

    _____

    _____

    _____

    _____

    _____

34. **Model:** She offered her roommate the car.
    Sample Imitation: I prepared my brother a sandwich.
    Your Imitations:

    _____

    _____

    _____

    _____

    _____

35. **Model:** <u>The</u> company made <u>the</u> manager <u>a</u> fine offer.
    Sample Imitation: The crew built the couple a comfortable house.
    Your Imitations:

    _____

    _____

    _____

    _____

    _____

36. **Model:** Amanda <u>has</u> enjoyed the play.
    Sample Imitation: The firefighter has given his life.
    Your Imitations:

    _____

    _____

    _____

    _____

    _____

37. **Model:** The movie <u>has</u> <u>not</u> <u>yet</u> begun.
    Sample Imitation: The crew has not yet eaten.
    Your Imitations:

    _____

    _____

    _____

    _____

    _____

38. **Model:** My parents <u>have</u> already met my boyfriend.
    Sample Imitation: The journalists have never proved their story.
    Your Imitations:

    _____

    _____

    _____

    _____

    _____

39. **Model:** The cruise ship <u>will</u> maintain a regular entertainment schedule.
    Sample Imitation: The new president will convene an immediate emergency meeting.
    Your Imitations:

    _____

    _____

    _____

    _____

    _____

40. **Model:** The babies <u>will</u> <u>not</u> receive <u>their</u> usual shots.
    Sample Imitation: The truckers will not unload their precious cargo.
    Your Imitations:

    _____

    _____

    _____

    _____

41. **Model:** You <u>must</u> have liked the food.
    Sample Imitation: They must have preferred the country.
    Your Imitations:

    _____

    _____

    _____

    _____

    _____

42. **Model:** The medical examiner <u>had</u> <u>not</u> delivered his report.
    Sample Imitation: The toddler had not soiled his pants.
    Your Imitations:

    _____

    _____

    _____

    _____

    _____

43. **Model:** The pilot <u>might</u> have landed the plane safely.
    Sample Imitation: The medicine might have started the healing slowly.
    Your Imitations:

    _____

    _____

    _____

    _____

    _____

44. **Model:** The wedding coordinators <u>could</u> have done a better job.
    Sample Imitation: The office janitors could have overheard a nasty rumor.
    Your Imitations:

    _____

    _____

    _____

    _____

    _____

45. **Model:** These dark clouds <u>might</u> bring much rain tomorrow.
    Sample Imitation: Those antique dolls might fetch a high price this afternoon.
    Your Imitations:

    _____

    _____

    _____

    _____

    _____

46. **Model:** They <u>would</u> not return the favor.
    Sample Imitation: She would not answer the questions.
    Your Imitations:

    _____

    _____

    _____

    _____

    _____

47. **Model:** Schools <u>should</u> not teach sex education.
    Sample Imitation: Gardeners should not move delicate plants.
    Your Imitations:

    _____

    _____

    _____

    _____

    _____

48. **Model:** The passengers <u>can</u> choose their seats.
    Sample Imitation: The students can bring their dictionary.
    Your Imitations:

    _____

    _____

    _____

    _____

    _____

49. **Model:** Cows <u>cannot</u> always supply milk.

    Sample Imitation: Doctors cannot often take vacations.

    Your Imitations:

    _____

    _____

    _____

    _____

    _____

50. **Model:** <u>Do</u> you understand the lesson?

    Sample Imitation: Do they run the show?

    Your Imitations:

    _____

    _____

    _____

    _____

    _____

51. **Model:** <u>Did</u> the supervisor make a mistake?

    Sample Imitation: Did the pilots crash the plane?

    Your Imitations:

    _____

    _____

    _____

    _____

    _____

52. **Model:** <u>Did</u> you <u>not</u> hear me?

    Sample Imitation: Did I not tell you?

    Your Imitations:

    _____

    _____

    _____

    _____

    _____

53. **Model:** <u>Do</u> <u>not</u> make a scene.
    Sample Imitation: Do not hurt the child.
    Your Imitations:

    _____

    _____

    _____

    _____

54. **Model:** <u>Does</u> it drop its leaves?
    Sample Imitation: Does he fake his tears?
    Your Imitations:

    _____

    _____

    _____

    _____

55. **Model:** <u>Does</u> she <u>not</u> have an umbrella?
    Sample Imitation: Does he not carry a gun?
    Your Imitations:

    _____

    _____

    _____

    _____

56. **Model:** The president <u>may</u> <u>have</u> known for days.
    Sample Imitation: The consumers may have complained for nothing.
    Your Imitations:

    _____

    _____

    _____

    _____

57. **Model:** The contractors <u>should</u> <u>have</u> given an exact completion date.

Sample Imitation: The counselors should have made a more appropriate remark.

Your Imitations:

_____

_____

_____

_____

58. **Model:** <u>Will</u> you please answer my question?

Sample Imitation: Will they finally release the keys?

Your Imitations:

_____

_____

_____

_____

59. **Model:** My parents <u>might</u> <u>not</u> believe me.

Sample Imitation: Your sister might not trust you.

Your Imitations:

_____

_____

_____

_____

WORKSHOP C—SIMPLE SENTENCES WITH INTRODUCTORY PHRASES AND PREPOSITIONS

In this workshop, change all the words except the ones that are underlined. Keep the sentence structure.

1. Yesterday, the girl bought a new dress at Macy's.
   Earlier, the boy met a good friend at the park.

   _____

   _____

   _____

   _____

   _____

2. In the morning, we like toast and coffee for breakfast.

   _____

   _____

   _____

   _____

   _____

   _____

3. At the fair, he won several prizes for his friend.

   _____

   _____

   _____

   _____

   _____

   _____

4. Before class, she enjoys a short nap in the library.

   _____

   _____

   _____

   _____

   _____

5. <u>Until</u> today, I exercised thirty minutes each morning <u>in</u> my home gym.

_____

_____

_____

_____

_____

6. Last night, I did not sleep a wink <u>until</u> dawn.

_____

_____

_____

_____

7. Every day, they eat dinner <u>with</u> their entire family.

_____

_____

_____

_____

8. Every summer, my brothers <u>and</u> I spent a long weekend <u>at</u> the river.

_____

_____

_____

_____

9. Yesterday afternoon, they drank their coffee quietly <u>at</u> the table.

_____

_____

_____

_____

_____

10. Every month, she pays her bills <u>on</u> the first.

_____

_____

_____

_____

_____

11. <u>At</u> the park, the mischievous children peeked <u>around</u> the corner.

_____

_____

_____

_____

_____

12. <u>By</u> the end of the day, I usually enjoy <u>a</u> long bath and my favorite novel.

_____

_____

_____

_____

_____

13. <u>After</u> dinner, we will watch a movie.

_____

_____

_____

_____

_____

14. <u>After</u> her swim, she went <u>to</u> her room <u>to</u> study.

_____

_____

_____

_____

15. Forever grateful, <u>the</u> family wrote <u>a</u> long letter <u>of</u> thanks.

_____

_____

_____

_____

16. <u>In</u> our new house, we all have private space.

_____

_____

_____

_____

_____

17. <u>On</u> weekends, we usually relax <u>and</u> play <u>with</u> our children.

_____

_____

_____

_____

_____

18. <u>After</u> dinner, the kids will go <u>to</u> the movies.

_____

_____

_____

_____

_____

19. Every Saturday, the game starts <u>at</u> three o' clock.

_____

_____

_____

_____

_____

20. <u>In</u> my opinion, <u>the</u> chair <u>at</u> my office is not very comfortable.

_____

_____

_____

_____

_____

21. <u>In</u> the hospital, a nurse <u>with</u> nice bedside manners took care <u>of</u> me.

_____

_____

_____

_____

_____

22. Undoubtedly, some fashion magazines claim <u>to</u> stand as practical guides <u>for</u> the American girl.

_____

_____

_____

_____

_____

23. <u>After</u> clos<u>ing</u> the deal, the salesman gave him the keys <u>to</u> his new car.

_____

_____

_____

_____

_____

WORKSHOP D—SIMPLE SENTENCES WITH LINKING VERBS (STATE OF BEING VERBS)

In this workshop, change all the words except the underlined linking verb. Keep the sentence structure.

1. The girls <u>are</u> happy.

_____

_____

_____

_____

_____

_____

2. The food <u>is</u> poisonous.

_____

_____

_____

_____

_____

_____

3. Harry <u>is</u> my favorite uncle.

_____

_____

_____

_____

_____

_____

4. My aunt Janice <u>is</u> a lovely person.

_____

_____

_____

_____

_____

_____

5. Jodi <u>is</u> not as glamorous as my other friends.

_____

_____

_____

_____

_____

6. My favorite hobby <u>is</u> to hike in the mountains.

_____

_____

_____

_____

_____

7. Every family, at one time or another, <u>is</u> confronted with the terminal illness of one of its members.

_____

_____

_____

_____

_____

8. Both the movie and the book <u>are</u> interesting.

_____

_____

_____

_____

_____

9. The party <u>was</u> enjoyable.

_____

_____

_____

_____

_____

_____

10. The scene of the accident <u>has</u> <u>been</u> cleared.

_____

_____

_____

_____

_____

11. This year's football team <u>has</u> <u>been</u> a huge disappointment.

_____

_____

_____

_____

_____

12. She <u>seemed</u> alarmed.

_____

_____

_____

_____

_____

13. You <u>seem</u> totally immersed in the novel.

_____

_____

_____

_____

_____

14. She <u>appears</u> strong <u>enough</u> to lift this box.

_____

_____

_____

_____

_____

15. He <u>appears</u> brave <u>enough</u> to face the snarling dog.

_____

_____

_____

_____

_____

16. My daughter <u>appeared</u> pleased at the news.

_____

_____

_____

_____

_____

17. You <u>appeared</u> quite relaxed during your speech.

_____

_____

_____

_____

_____

18. My elderly grandmother <u>remains</u> active.

_____

_____

_____

_____

_____

19. The facts <u>remain</u> undisputed.

_____

_____

_____

_____

_____

20. My young son <u>remains</u> active in sports.

_____

_____

_____

_____

_____

21. The official documents <u>remained</u> confidential.

_____

_____

_____

_____

_____

22. The children <u>become</u> sleepy.

_____

_____

_____

_____

_____

23. My high school friend <u>became</u> a successful artist.

_____

_____

_____

_____

_____

24. They <u>look</u> exhausted after the long trip.

_____

_____

_____

_____

_____

25. I <u>look</u> good in my evening gown.

_____

_____

_____

_____

_____

26. You <u>looked</u> sad at the ceremony.

_____

_____

_____

_____

_____

27. The girl <u>grew</u> suspicious of her friend.

_____

_____

_____

_____

_____

28. We <u>were</u> slowly <u>growing</u> impatient with the discussion.

_____

_____

_____

_____

_____

29. Her face <u>turns</u> green with envy.

_____

_____

_____

_____

_____

_____

30. The milk <u>turned</u> sour overnight.

_____

_____

_____

_____

_____

31. You <u>appeared</u> happy with all your presents.

_____

_____

_____

_____

_____

32. The candidate <u>appears</u> confident in her winning.

_____

_____

_____

_____

_____

_____

33. It <u>gets</u> chilly in the evening.

_____

_____

_____

_____

_____

34. My parents <u>got</u> upset again.

_____

_____

_____

_____

_____

35. Somehow, this does not <u>feel</u> right.

_____

_____

_____

_____

_____

36. My sister <u>felt</u> excited about her new baby.

_____

_____

_____

_____

_____

37. The fabric <u>feels</u> very soft.

_____

_____

_____

_____

_____

_____

38. The chicken farm in my neighborhood <u>smells</u> horrible.

_____

_____

_____

_____

_____

_____

39. The house <u>smells</u> sweet with the fresh flowers.

_____

_____

_____

_____

_____

_____

40. Nicky <u>sounded</u> doubtful of the plan's success.

_____

_____

_____

_____

_____

_____

41. The band <u>will</u> <u>sound</u> better than ever tomorrow.

_____

_____

_____

_____

_____

42. This dessert <u>tastes</u> like honey.

_____

_____

_____

_____

_____

43. The medicine <u>tasted</u> very bitter.

_____

_____

_____

_____

_____

44. My dear, you <u>fell</u> short of your goals.

_____

_____

_____

_____

_____

45. I often <u>fall</u> behind in my assignments.

_____

_____

_____

_____

_____

46. The scientists <u>will</u> <u>prove</u> successful in their research.

_____

_____

_____

_____

_____

47. The plan <u>proved</u> inadequate.

_____

_____

_____

_____

_____

48. Sometimes, my sister <u>runs</u> amok.

_____

_____

_____

_____

_____

49. Don't <u>get</u> funny with me.

_____

_____

_____

_____

_____

50. You <u>get</u> so upset for nothing!

_____

_____

_____

_____

_____

51. I <u>stayed</u> put all morning.

_____

_____

_____

_____

_____

52. Please <u>stay</u> calm.

_____

_____

_____

_____

_____

53. I want her <u>to</u> <u>lie</u> still for the compress application.

_____

_____

_____

_____

_____

54. The beautiful flowers <u>lay</u> all over the coffin.

_____

_____

_____

_____

_____

_____

WORKSHOP E—SIMPLE SENTENCES WITH INTRANSITIVE VERBS

In this workshop, keep the underlined verb; change everything else. Maintain the sentence structure.

1. **Model:** The hikers <u>struggled</u> up the mountain peak.
    Sample Imitation: The old woman struggled in the narrow street.
    Your Imitations:

    _____

    _____

    _____

    _____

    _____

    _____

2. **Model:** On Thanksgiving Day, the whole family <u>ate</u> heartily.
    Sample Imitation: At the community fair, all the children ate frantically.
    Your Imitations:

    _____

    _____

    _____

    _____

    _____

    _____

3. **Model:** Plants <u>thrive</u> in the right location.
    Sample Imitation: Children thrive with caring parents.
    Your Imitations:

    _____

    _____

    _____

    _____

    _____

4. **Model:** The speaker's voice <u>carried</u> through the huge auditorium.
   Sample Imitation: The airplanes' sounds carried through the open countryside.
   Your Imitations:

   _____

   _____

   _____

   _____

   _____

5. **Model:** His relatives from Australia <u>arrived</u> two days late.
   Sample Imitation: Our presents from Europe arrived after Christmas.
   Your Imitations:

   _____

   _____

   _____

   _____

   _____

6. **Model:** The medical students <u>watched</u> during the long autopsy.
   Sample Imitation: The proud parents watched at the play rehearsal.
   Your Imitations:

   _____

   _____

   _____

   _____

   _____

7. **Model:** We will <u>leave</u> now.
    Sample Imitation: She must leave soon.
    Your Imitations:

    _____

    _____

    _____

    _____

    _____

8. **Model:** The performers <u>move</u> constantly across the stage.
    Sample Imitation: The crowds move frantically towards the White House.
    Your Imitations:

    _____

    _____

    _____

    _____

    _____

9. **Model:** The customers <u>lingered</u> a while <u>after</u> the show.
    Sample Imitation: The witness lingered some time after the accident.
    Your Imitations:

    _____

    _____

    _____

    _____

    _____

10. **Model:** The energetic teenagers <u>dance</u> frantically.
    Sample Imitation: The older people dance softly.
    Your Imitations:

    _____

    _____

    _____

    _____

WORKSHOP F—SIMPLE SENTENCES WITH GERUNDS AND PRESENT PARTICIPLES

In this workshop, change all the words but use gerunds and present participles as they are used in the models.

1. The thundering storm moved in quickly, darkening the sky and flooding the streets.

_____

_____

_____

_____

_____

_____

2. Pulling his coat over his head, the old man quickly moved away into the night.

_____

_____

_____

_____

_____

3. Carrying their heavy textbooks, the students made their way to their classrooms.

_____

_____

_____

_____

_____

4. Keeping one eye on the baby, the mother finished preparing the meal.

_____

_____

_____

_____

_____

5. Linda lifted the puppy and, caressing it, placed it gently in the basket.

_____

_____

_____

_____

_____

_____

6. The tiger attacked its prey, breaking its neck, and dragged it under cover.

_____

_____

_____

_____

_____

7. The tiger attacked its prey and, breaking its neck, dragged it under cover.

_____

_____

_____

_____

_____

8. Going on fad diets deceives many about their weight problems.

_____

_____

_____

_____

_____

_____

9. Making paper by hand became an art, lost long ago and revived recently.

_____

_____

_____

_____

_____

10. Destroying the diary was his worst mistake.

_____

_____

_____

_____

_____

11. Having waited ten years for this opportunity, Juan wholeheartedly immersed himself in his new career.

_____

_____

_____

_____

_____

12. Juan wholeheartedly immersed himself in his new career, having waited ten years for this opportunity.

_____

_____

_____

_____

_____

13. Juan, having waited ten years for this opportunity, wholeheartedly immersed himself in his new career.

_____

_____

_____

_____

_____

_____

14. Shy people might try joining clubs and participating in small group activities.

_____

_____

_____

_____

_____

_____

15. The workability program helps high school students find jobs by introducing them to prospective employers.

_____

_____

_____

_____

_____

_____

16. Studying his position, planning his strategy, and anticipating the probabilities, the chess player finally makes his move.

_____

_____

_____

_____

_____

_____

17. Keeping an eye on the instructor, Chris glanced at the magazine hidden under his desk, hoping not to get caught.

_____

_____

_____

_____

_____

18. Feeling uncertain about the future, Jamie consulted several friends and decided what to do next.

_____

_____

_____

_____

_____

19. Buying a new car can be a stressful adventure.

_____

_____

_____

_____

_____

20. We completed setting up the banquet table by carefully placing the napkins and the silverware.

_____

_____

_____

_____

_____

21. The parents' job is keeping their children in good health and safe and teaching them the difference between right and wrong.

_____

_____

_____

_____

_____

22. By putting a little money aside every month, he finally succeeded in getting the car he wanted.

_____

_____

_____

_____

_____

23. Begin the test by carefully reading the directions.

_____

_____

_____

_____

_____

24. Keeping finances in order throughout the year prevents great headaches at income tax time.

_____

_____

_____

_____

_____

25. Admiring the sculpture, a visitor to the exhibit decided to try his hand at sculpting.

_____

_____

_____

_____

_____

_____

26. Will you consider running for office next year?

_____

_____

_____

_____

_____

_____

27. My daughter's responsibility this weekend is feeding the pets and cleaning their pan.

_____

_____

_____

_____

_____

_____

28. Finding the noise unbearable, I finally left the room.

_____

_____

_____

_____

_____

_____

29. Her father, being a war veteran, had many fascinating stories to tell.

_____

_____

_____

_____

_____

_____

30. Courtney, having lost her way, stopped and asked a gas station attendant.

_____

_____

_____

_____

_____

_____

31. Having registered for several heavy courses, Joshua began wondering what this semester would be like.

_____

_____

_____

_____

_____

_____

32. Knowing that snacks and fast food are unhealthy does not prevent my sister from eating them regularly.

_____

_____

_____

_____

_____

_____

33. Finding the classroom empty, Gil turned around and went to see a friend.

_____

_____

_____

_____

_____

34. A child wearing a Halloween mask went from door to door scaring everyone.

_____

_____

_____

_____

_____

35. Keeping one foot on the pedal, the little girl continued riding her bike.

_____

_____

_____

_____

_____

36. In defusing the live bomb, the squad handled a delicate situation efficiently.

_____

_____

_____

_____

_____

WORKSHOP G—SIMPLE SENTENCES WITH PAST PARTICIPLES

In this workshop, change all the words but use past participles as they are used in the models.

1. Dazzled by the politician's speech, the crowd cheered.

_____

_____

_____

_____

_____

_____

2. Public schools, plagued by rebellion and violence, are forced to consider safety measures.

_____

_____

_____

_____

_____

_____

3. Plagued by rebellion and violence, public schools are forced to consider safety measures.

_____

_____

_____

_____

_____

_____

4. My parents, attracted by a better life in America, are waiting for a visa.

_____

_____

_____

_____

_____

_____

5. The accountants, highly recommended, are conducting the audit for our firm.

_____

_____

_____

_____

_____

6. Born in Atlanta in a family of twelve, she brought with her a rich background.

_____

_____

_____

_____

_____

7. Broken up by the news of her mother's passing, she retreated from the company of her friends.

_____

_____

_____

_____

_____

8. Known for her love of gossip, her friends do not always tell her everything.

_____

_____

_____

_____

_____

9. Carefully bred, the puppies demonstrated the qualities desired by their owner.

_____

_____

_____

_____

_____

10. Burned to a crisp, the burgers had to be thrown out.

_____

_____

_____

_____

_____

11. Caught in the act, the burglars had no time to escape.

_____

_____

_____

_____

_____

12. Sentenced to death, the prisoner showed no emotion.

_____

_____

_____

_____

_____

13. Alarmed by the change in her expression, he promptly stopped talking.

_____

_____

_____

_____

_____

_____

14. The students, prompted by the proctors, started the standardized test.

_____

_____

_____

_____

_____

15. Angered by her sister's words, she went out for a walk.

_____

_____

_____

_____

_____

16. Maria, stunningly dressed for the prom, posed for the photographer.

_____

_____

_____

_____

_____

17. Determined to succeed in math, Jesse spent many evenings studying and practicing his lessons.

_____

_____

_____

_____

_____

18. Mismanaged for years, the company finally went bankrupt.

_____

_____

_____

_____

_____

19. The painting, started hours ago, seemed no closer to being finished.

_____

_____

_____

_____

_____

20. Irritated with the presidential candidates, many citizens decided not to vote.

_____

_____

_____

_____

_____

_____

21. In a carefully controlled tone, he explained his unhappiness.

_____

_____

_____

_____

_____

22. Finally gone, the house guests left me tired and happy to be alone.

_____

_____

_____

_____

_____

23. Thrown in the ocean by the hurricane, the car was totally destroyed.

_____

_____

_____

_____

_____

24. Stricken with grief, the family attempted to regain some normalcy in their life.

_____

_____

_____

_____

_____

25. Completely equipped for a mountain hike, the team set off at dawn.

_____

_____

_____

_____

_____

26. His mother, drenched by the heavy rain, quickly climbed into a cab.

_____

_____

_____

_____

_____

27. The architects, very skilled, designed a new bedroom for my son.

_____

_____

_____

_____

_____

28. Educated in California, in a prestigious school, she led a good life.

_____

_____

_____

_____

_____

29. All opinions having been heard, the meeting was finally adjourned.

_____

_____

_____

_____

_____

_____

WORKSHOP H—COMPOUND SENTENCES WITH COORDINATING CONJUNCTIONS

In this workshop, change all the words except the coordinating conjunction. In this workshop, you may also take some liberties with the sentence structure as long as you maintain the coordinating structure and punctuation.

1. Bryan likes football, and he practices every day.
   My parrot is funny, and he makes me laugh.

   _____

   _____

   _____

   _____

   _____

2. Bryan likes football and practices every day.
   My parrot is funny and makes me laugh.

   _____

   _____

   _____

   _____

   _____

3. My car is old, yet it runs well.

   _____

   _____

   _____

   _____

   _____

4. Larry works hard, but he always takes time to read.

_____

_____

_____

_____

_____

5. We can cook dinner at home, or we can order pizza.

_____

_____

_____

_____

_____

6. I found a stray dog, so I brought it home and named it Gunther.

_____

_____

_____

_____

_____

7. I understand a lot about computers, but my parents do not.

_____

_____

_____

_____

_____

8. Jeff likes school, yet he struggles to get to class on time.

_____

_____

_____

_____

_____

9. He likes to debate, but his friends do not.

_____

_____

_____

_____

_____

10. They can watch a movie at home or go to the bowling alley.

_____

_____

_____

_____

_____

11. The spaniel fetched the stick and brought it to his master.

_____

_____

_____

_____

_____

12. I have seen this movie three times, yet I still enjoy every minute of it.

_____

_____

_____

_____

_____

13. You can refinance your home, but be careful to choose the right loan.

_____

_____

_____

_____

_____

14. We cannot visit you next week, nor can we take the day off.

_____

_____

_____

_____

_____

15. Daniel should leave two hours early, or he might arrive too late at the airport.

_____

_____

_____

_____

_____

16. Yolanda has not stopped crying, nor does she show signs of feeling better.

_____

_____

_____

_____

_____

17. Daniel would like a great career in law, yet he does not want to be in school for years.

_____

_____

_____

_____

_____

18. The company managers held a meeting, for they knew the workers had some complaints.

_____

_____

_____

_____

_____

19. My brother and his friends ate early, for they wanted to go to baseball practice.

_____

_____

_____

_____

_____

20. Neither my father nor my mother had much schooling.

_____

_____

_____

_____

_____

_____

21. Not only did I bruise my leg in the fall but I also broke my little finger.

_____

_____

_____

_____

_____

_____

22. Both his sister and his brother dropped out of high school.

_____

_____

_____

_____

_____

_____

23. Whether you like it or not, this is what we are going to do.

_____

_____

_____

_____

_____

_____

WORKSHOP I—COMPLEX SENTENCES WITH SUBORDINATING CONJUNCTIONS

In this workshop, keep the subordinating conjunction. Change all the other words. In this workshop, you may also take some liberties with the sentence structure as long as you maintain the subordinating structure and punctuation.

1. Before you leave the house, turn off all the lights.
   Before you go to sleep, open all the windows.

   _____

   _____

   _____

   _____

   _____

   _____

2. Turn off all the lights before you leave the house.
   Open all the windows before you go to sleep.

   _____

   _____

   _____

   _____

   _____

   _____

3. Before you say something mean, think about it.

   _____

   _____

   _____

   _____

   _____

   _____

4. Before they leave the baseball field, they program all the sprinklers.

_____

_____

_____

_____

_____

_____

5. All conversations cease when she starts singing.
   Everyone is scared when he drives his car.

_____

_____

_____

_____

_____

_____

6. Unless you hurry, we will be late.
   Unless I pay the rent, I will be evicted.

_____

_____

_____

_____

_____

_____

7. Since he is doing an excellent job, he will receive a bonus.
   Since the elevator does not work, we will have to take the stairs.

_____

_____

_____

_____

_____

_____

8. The phone rang while I was checking the messages.
   While I stood outside waiting for my friend, the movie started.

   _____

   _____

   _____

   _____

   _____

9. If it rains, the graduation exercises will be held in the auditorium.

   _____

   _____

   _____

   _____

   _____

10. I play drums once in a while although I prefer to play the guitar.
    I do not feel ready for the test although I studied for hours.

    _____

    _____

    _____

    _____

    _____

11. Because my son was sick yesterday, I stayed home and kept him company.
    Because my friend was lonely tonight, I remained close and gave him support.

    _____

    _____

    _____

    _____

    _____

    _____

With the next sentences, note the order of the words if you reverse them.

12. I stayed home and kept my son company yesterday because he was sick.
    I remained close and gave my friend support tonight because he was lonely.

_____

_____

_____

_____

_____

_____

13. I plan to buy a new car because this one is getting old.

_____

_____

_____

_____

_____

_____

14. As I grew older, I started to understand myself better.

_____

_____

_____

_____

_____

_____

15. Whenever the rainy season starts, I catch one cold after the other.

_____

_____

_____

_____

_____

_____

16. As long as she is going out, she could pick up the prescription.

_____

_____

_____

_____

_____

17. Once I understood the lesson, I did very well on all the tests.

_____

_____

_____

_____

_____

18. Until you do your chores, you cannot go out to the arcade.

_____

_____

_____

_____

_____

19. Now that we have the Internet, students can do research at home.

_____

_____

_____

_____

_____

20. As soon as your car repair is done, we will call you.

_____

_____

_____

_____

_____

21. Where you go, I will follow.

_____

_____

_____

_____

_____

22. I study all weekend so that I pass the final exam.

_____

_____

_____

_____

_____

23. People lost a lot of money due to the market crash.

_____

_____

_____

_____

_____

24. I occasionally go to restaurants even though I do not like to go out.

_____

_____

_____

_____

_____

25. Whereas you enjoy skiing, I prefer mountain hiking.

_____

_____

_____

_____

_____

26. Rather than risking a parking ticket, go around the block to find a space.

_____

_____

_____

_____

_____

27. If only my brother had not been so lazy, he would have a career by now.

_____

_____

_____

_____

_____

28. Whether the storm clears or not, I am going on my walk.

_____

_____

_____

_____

_____

_____

29. Even if you pay me, I will not eat that concoction.

_____

_____

_____

_____

_____

_____

WORKSHOP J—COMPLEX SENTENCES WITH RELATIVE PRONOUNS

In this workshop, keep the relative pronoun. Change everything else but maintain the sentence structure.

Relative Pronoun "Who"

1. The man who is president of the bank is my father.
   The girl who is cashier at Barnes & Noble is a friend.

   _____

   _____

   _____

   _____

   _____

   _____

2. The architect who designed this house has a great sense of space.

   _____

   _____

   _____

   _____

   _____

   _____

3. My father, who is president of the bank, comes home late every night.
   My sister, who is a kindergarten teacher, plays with the children each morning.

   _____

   _____

   _____

   _____

   _____

   _____

4. These people, who live in a glass house, do not value privacy.
   The couple, who bought the portrait, do not intend to display it.

   _____

   _____

   _____

   _____

   _____

   _____

5. The football coach who is well known in town was arrested.
   The nurses who treated my head were very compassionate.

   _____

   _____

   _____

   _____

   _____

   _____

6. That nurse, who took care of me, has a nice bedside manner.
   My boyfriend, who is leader of the club, runs every morning.

   _____

   _____

   _____

   _____

   _____

   _____

7. The cook who prepared this dish has a passion for eggplant.

   _____

   _____

   _____

   _____

   _____

   _____

8. The soccer players, who have performed well, are waiting to receive a gold medal.
   The new students, who have just arrived, are hoping to get their class schedule.

   _____

   _____

   _____

   _____

   _____

9. Students who do not study do not learn.
   People who do not respect others do not have friends.

   _____

   _____

   _____

   _____

   _____

Relative Pronoun "That"

10. The keys that you lost have been found in the taxi.
    The shirt that you bought looks just like mine.

    _____

    _____

    _____

    _____

    _____

11. The book that you requested is out of print.
    The paragraphs that you created have been read in class.

    _____

    _____

    _____

    _____

    _____

12. The shoes that I wore at the wedding were too tight.
    The horse that I rode at the fair was very slow.

_____

_____

_____

_____

_____

_____

In all the previous sentences, it is acceptable to not write the word that. *However, it is necessary to know that the word is implied.*

EXAMPLES

The horse I rode at the fair was very slow.
The paragraphs you created have been read in class.
In some of the following examples, it is best to retain the word that.

Note the difference: The previous sentences start with a noun; the following sentences start with a verb.

13. We want a machine that is practical to use.
    I want a car that goes fast.

_____

_____

_____

_____

_____

_____

14. It was apparent that the politician was lying.
    It was remarkable that the child was walking.

_____

_____

_____

_____

_____

_____

15. She bought a sofa that is extremely comfortable.
     My uncle ran a debt that is truly unbelievable.

_____

_____

_____

_____

_____

Relative Pronoun "Which"

16. The camera, which I wanted so much, was too expensive.
     Gasoline, which smells so bad, should not be inhaled.

_____

_____

_____

_____

_____

17. The garden, which is open to the public, is expensive to maintain.
     Soda, which is consumed all over the world, has no nutrients.

_____

_____

_____

_____

_____

_____

18. Whale oil, which burns brightly, provided light in early American homes.
    Fresh bread, which tastes delicious, attracted people in the morning hours.

    _____

    _____

    _____

    _____

    _____

    _____

19. Surfing, which is so popular in Hawaii, generates much business.

    _____

    _____

    _____

    _____

    _____

    _____

20. The director gave me the part of Juliet, which I consider quite an honor.
    The artist drew Eric a picture of us, which he accepted with extreme gratitude.

    _____

    _____

    _____

    _____

    _____

    _____

WORKSHOP K—COMPLEX SENTENCES
WITH CONJUNCTIVE ADVERBS

In this workshop, change all the words except the conjunctive adverb.

1. Tommy did not learn to swim until he was fifteen; however, he made the Olympic team.
    I learned to drive when I was twelve; however, I did not get my license until I was fifteen.

    _____

    _____

    _____

    _____

    _____

2. The weather deteriorated quickly; therefore, the picnic was cancelled.
    My friend felt dizzy; therefore, we took her to the hospital.

    _____

    _____

    _____

    _____

    _____

3. Naomi has big plans for her future; meanwhile, she concentrates on doing well in school.

    _____

    _____

    _____

    _____

    _____

    _____

4. Caitlin enjoys browsing in clothing stores; as a result, she spends a lot of money on new outfits.

_____

_____

_____

_____

_____

_____

5. This is a very bad idea; also, it makes me wonder if I can trust him.

_____

_____

_____

_____

_____

_____

6. My grandmother Lola is a wonderful woman; besides, she is a talented singer.

_____

_____

_____

_____

_____

7. The financing company gave my sister a good loan; in addition, they gave her the lowest interest rate available.

_____

_____

_____

_____

_____

_____

8. Rick's dog was hit by a car and died; then, Rick buried him in his yard.

_____

_____

_____

_____

_____

_____

9. The concert did not start on time; in fact, we sat and waited two hours.
The children were in shock after the accident; in fact, they could not concentrate in school for two weeks.

_____

_____

_____

_____

_____

_____

10. Many prescribed drugs do more harm than good; for example, their side effects are often worse than their benefits.

_____

_____

_____

_____

_____

11. Kids often do not like to help around the house; nevertheless, they need to contribute.

_____

_____

_____

_____

_____

_____

12. Please, tell your friend to hurry; otherwise, we will miss the plane.
    Mark does not seem to understand what we are talking about; otherwise, he would not look so lost.

_____

_____

_____

_____

_____

_____

13. My sister thought she was going to Australia next summer; instead, it turns out she will go to Mexico.

_____

_____

_____

_____

_____

_____

14. I like snow; on the other hand, I like hot summer days even better.

_____

_____

_____

_____

_____

15. The funeral was over; afterwards, the family had a meal together.

_____

_____

_____

_____

_____

_____

16. I was not home when the delivery van arrived; consequently, I did not get my new sofa that day.

_____

_____

_____

_____

_____

17. The young girl was troubled; indeed, she cried often.

_____

_____

_____

_____

_____

18. Chris prepared all the ingredients; next, she started mixing the batter.

_____

_____

_____

_____

_____

19. Eat your dinner; later, you can have some ice cream.

_____

_____

_____

_____

_____

Note a special use of the conjunctive adverb in the following sentences.

20. Bill and Jane would not dream, of course, of eloping to Las Vegas.

_____

_____

_____

_____

_____

_____

21. The rain had stopped. The slope, however, continued to slide until morning.

_____

_____

_____

_____

_____

_____

WORKSHOP L—COMPLEX/COMPOUND SENTENCES

In this workshop, change all the words but keep the coordinating conjunctions and the subordinating conjunctions, relative pronouns, or conjunctive adverbs.

1. On any weekend, Jack can quite easily sleep all day or, if he is particularly energetic, arise before noon.

   _____

   _____

   _____

   _____

   _____

2. One of the functions of the wilderness is to teach us that constant activity is not the only useful way of life, but some people neglect rest and recreation.

   _____

   _____

   _____

   _____

   _____

3. As I walked slowly into the forest, past the fields and the farm buildings, the air became cooler, and the day became dusk.

   _____

   _____

   _____

   _____

   _____

4. Efficient use of time and resources is vital for college students who want to not only succeed in their classes but also find time to relax.

_____

_____

_____

_____

_____

_____

5. Before the high school prom, the re-enaction of an automobile crash with drunk teenagers intended to bring home the horrific consequences of drinking and driving, and it emphasized the need for personal responsibility.

_____

_____

_____

_____

_____

_____

6. During their recent family crisis, the brothers remained strong and took care of their young siblings since they had no relatives left in the world.

_____

_____

_____

_____

_____

_____

7. While Juan can play several musical instruments, he nevertheless rarely performs, and his friends think it is a waste of wonderful talent.

_____

_____

_____

_____

_____

_____

8. Although he knows how to parallel park, he hates to do it, gets nervous, and inevitably hits the curb or the car in front.

_____

_____

_____

_____

_____

9. In warehouses, employees who have been hired as forklift operators must be extensively trained, and they must be aware of safety issues.

_____

_____

_____

_____

_____

10. In spite of the fact that we were much too tired to continue with the move, we felt anxious to sit in a comfortable living room, so we put in the extra effort.

_____

_____

_____

_____

_____

_____

4

PHRASE COMBINING: FROM RANDOM THOUGHTS TO POLISHED PARAGRAPHS

This chapter describes an efficient strategy to successfully engage in the writing process. It may seem tedious at first, but this method leads to well-written paragraphs faster than any other.

- Step One: *Jot down words and short phrases about your subject or topic.*
  student, begin homework, nap, desk, books

- Step Two: *Write short sentences in a logical sequence.*
  The student woke from a refreshing nap.
  The student gathered his books.
  The student sat at his desk.
  The student began his homework.

- Step Three: *Make a selection of various conjunctions, prepositions, and other connecting words and punctuation symbols and use them according to the structures that have been practiced in Chapter 3.*
  The student woke from a refreshing nap, gathered his books, sat at his desk, and began his homework.
  The student woke from a refreshing nap, gathered his books, and sat at his desk to start his homework.
  After waking from a refreshing nap and gathering his books, the student sat at his desk and started his homework.
  The student woke from a refreshing nap and, gathering his books, sat at his desk to start his homework.
  The student woke from a refreshing nap and, gathering his books, he sat at his desk and started his homework.
  The student started his homework after waking from a refreshing nap, gathering his books, and sitting at his desk.
  After waking from a refreshing nap, the student gathered his books and sat at his desk. He started his homework.
  The student started his homework; he had awakened from a refreshing nap, gathered his books, and sat at his desk.

It is possible to continue creating several additional variations of this simple sentence. For example, one could re-
place the word after *by the words* as soon as. *Changes like this increase the level of complexity and accuracy*
through subtle changes in meaning. The exercise obligates you to decide exactly what you wish to say.

EXAMPLE 1

lifeguard, waves, whistle, child, shift, distress

1. The lifeguard started his shift.
2. The lifeguard scanned the waves.
3. The lifeguard spotted a child in distress.
4. The lifeguard blew his whistle.
5. The lifeguard ran to save the boy.

Now, practice a variety of sentence structures, making a few changes in the wording without
changing the meaning. For example,

> As he started his shift, the lifeguard scanned the waves, spotted a child in distress, and, while
> blowing his whistle, he ran to save him.
> The lifeguard scanned the waves as he started his shift, and when he spotted a child in distress,
> he blew his whistle and ran to save her.
> While scanning the waves at the beginning of his shift, the lifeguard spotted a child in distress. He
> blew his whistle and ran to save him.
> Just as he started his shift and scanned the waves, the lifeguard spotted a child in distress. He
> blew his whistle while running to save the boy.
> The lifeguard blew his whistle and ran to save a boy. He had just started his shift and was
> scanning the waves when he spotted the child in distress.
> Running to save a boy, the lifeguard blew his whistle for he had spotted a child in distress while
> scanning the waves at the beginning of his shift.

Not only do exercises like the previous ones provide excellent mental gymnastics, but they are
much easier and more pleasant to do than learning grammar!

EXAMPLE 2

Suppose you want to talk about people who grow their own produce. You might first make the following list:
    gardeners, vegetables and fruits, home, winter, storage

Going through the steps described in Section 1, you can now create one lovely sentence by combining the information like this:
    many home gardeners store vegetables and fruits that are enjoyed during the winter months.

Once you have written this sentence, you may want to add to it or modify it to reflect your intended message. For
example, you may want to add to your list something about the growing process and where or how the produce is stored.
The longer your list, the more variety you can use in creating your sentences and the more interesting your piece of
writing. You may also start with a short manageable list, write the sentence, and add to it later.

EXAMPLE 3

students, pizzas, tired, last homework, English

The list can become:
    After having completed their last English homework assignment, the tired students ordered three
    extra large pizzas.
    The tired students ordered three large pizzas after having completed their last English homework
    assignment.

EXAMPLE 4 FOR A PARAGRAPH

Suppose you wish to write a paragraph about your childhood place of residence.

First, create a list of your thoughts as they come to you at random. It could be something like this:

I grew up on a farm

My parents' farm

A forest at the back of the farm

Farm is fifty acres of good land

Childhood memories

I left to go to school

Parents spent their whole life on the farm

It was my father's parents' farm

We cut firewood in the forest

My parents raised bees on farm

Good memories

I am not happy on farm now

It was in Southern Missouri

I grew up around 1950

I return to the farm

During vacation

I got used to the city

The city has entertainment

This is a good list. Notice that it answers many questions one might ask you about the place where you grew up. These questions are:

WHO

WHAT

WHERE

WHEN

HOW

WHY

Always remember to give information that answers these questions when you write a paragraph.

The next step is to organize your list in an order that follows the previous questions and incorporates some logical or chronological order. Let's do that by putting numbers on the list as follows:

1	I grew up on a farm
3	My parents' farm
7	A forest at the back of the farm
5	Farm is fifty acres of good land
11	Childhood memories
13	I left to go to school
12	Parents spent their whole life on the farm
4	It was my father's parents' farm
8	We cut firewood in the forest
9	My parents raised bees on farm
10	Good memories
16	I am not happy on farm now
6	It was in Southern Missouri
2	I grew up around 1950
14	I return to the farm

15   During vacation
17   I got used to the city
18   The city has entertainment

Use some flexibility when organizing these phrases, but remember that they must flow and make sense once written into a paragraph.
Now put these numbers in a logical order like this:
1   I grew up on a farm
2   I grew up around 1950
3   My parents' farm
4   It was my father's parents' farm
5   Farm is fifty acres of good land
6   It was in Southern Missouri
7   A forest at the back of the farm
8   We cut firewood in the forest
9   My parents raised bees on farm
10   Good memories
11   Childhood memories
12   Parents spent their whole life on the farm
13   I left to go to school
14   I return to the farm
15   During vacation
16   I am not happy on farm now
17   I got used to the city
18   The city has entertainment

Now, remembering some of the sentence patterns you practiced with earlier, you can write a simple and correct paragraph. Simply turn the short phrases above into complete sentences by making sure that each one makes complete sense by itself.

Since the phrases have been organized into a logical sequence, keep that sequence or stay very close to it when you write the sentences.

Here is an example of what you can write with the organized list:

Where I grew up

I grew up in the 1950s on my parents' farm that also belonged to my father's parents. The farm was fifty acres of good land in Southern Missouri. There was a forest at the back of the farm where we cut firewood. My parents also raised bees, and I had good childhood memories. My parents spent their whole life on the farm, but I left to go to school. I now return when I am on vacation, but I am not happy on the farm because I got used to the city and its entertainment.

Although short and simple, this paragraph illustrates simple sentences, coordinated sentences, and subordinated sentences.

As students feel comfortable with creating these simple pieces, they can venture into more detail, sophistication, and variety in the sentence structures that they choose.

Here is a second draft:

Where I grew up

I grew up in the 1950s on a farm that my parents inherited from my father's parents. The fifty acres of good land in Southern Missouri were surrounded by forests where we used to cut firewood for our comfort in the cool season. For years, my parents raised bees, and I have good childhood memories of helping them collect the honey, always having a lick or two before the jars were sealed.

Although my parents spent their entire life on the farm, they understood my desire to leave and go to school. I often return when I am on vacation because I still feel good about my childhood years, but I would not really be happy living there. The city, with its entertainment and its possibilities, have captured my imagination, and that is where I will make my future.

Once the first simple but correct paragraph has been written, it becomes much easier to add to it thus making it more interesting with descriptive detail and reflective comments.

To improve one's writing skills, it is important to start with simple sentence constructions and ensure that they are always correct before attempting more complex arrangements. The key to success is to internalize correct structures and patterns so that writing is always correct, no matter how simple.

VERBAL RHYTHM

Another important aspect of writing well is to understand verbal meaning and verbal rhythm. Words are the raw material used to construct sentences and create meaning. Some words provide a purely descriptive type of meaning. For instance, the words *tree*, *house*, *friendship*, *happy*, *angry*, *run*, *eat*, and many like these simply describe things, places, people, feelings, and actions. Good writing includes many descriptive details, but meaning is mostly derived from other types of words that define the how and why of things. These words bring reflection to one's writing, which is a necessary component of useful and effective communication.

For example, look at the following sentence:

EXAMPLE

The deep blue lake was surrounded by grassy meadows undulating in the breeze.

The sentence is descriptive of the natural environment. However, the description implies that someone has looked at this place and has noticed various things about it. Most likely, that person has acquired some feelings about the scene as well. The primary feeling might be one of serenity and aesthetic pleasure. Serenity might come from the softness of lines and from the breeze whereas aesthetic pleasure might come from the softness combined with the colors involved.

This explanation has already brought in a *how* and *why* element. In this example, it is a cause-and-effect element. The cause of the feeling of serenity is the softness of lines and the breeze. This can be turned around to say that the softness of lines and the soft breeze had the effect of producing a sense of serenity. One word to indicate a cause-and-effect connection is the word *because*, a subordinating conjunction.

We can add it to the sentence and say:

EXAMPLE

*I enjoyed the scenery and felt serene **because** the deep blue lake was surrounded by grassy meadows undulating in the breeze.*

This sentence has more meaning than the first one, but its rhythm is not very good. Other words exist that indicate cause and effect.
Let's try this:

EXAMPLE

*The deep blue lake was surrounded by grassy meadows undulating in the breeze, **so** I enjoyed the scenery and felt serene.*

We can also try this:

EXAMPLE

*The deep blue lake was surrounded by grassy meadows undulating in the breeze; **as a result,** I enjoyed the scenery and felt serene.*

By now, you have recognized sentence structures you have imitated in Chapter 1, using the correct punctuation.

All three sentences are correct. They use words that indicate cause and effect. However, do you have a preference for one over the others? The second version, using the word *so*, is a better version because it is lighter and has a smoother rhythm that the others. For that reason, it fits the poetic content of the sentence better.

EXAMPLE

Nevertheless, all the sentence structures above lack movement.

The movement that exists in the content of the sentence should ideally be reflected in the sentence structure as well. Let's try again:

EXAMPLE

The deep blue lake, surrounded by grassy meadows undulating in the breeze, filled me with pleasurable serenity.

Or,

EXAMPLE

Standing by the deep blue lake, I had a sense of pleasurable serenity fill me slowly, surrounded as I was by grassy meadows undulating in the breeze.

Or,

EXAMPLE

The deep blue lake surrounded by grassy meadows undulating in the breeze and the clear sky punctuated by a few patchy clouds instilled in me a wonderful sense of serenity.

In order to hear and feel the rhythm of a sentence, one must practice reading it aloud many times, preferably in front of an audience. *The rhythm of a sentence is very important to the quality of writing. It is created with punctuation and the choice of words.* The rhythm of a sentence also helps others understand its components and meaning. The choice of words and the length of the sentence depend on what you wish to say. In a descriptive sentence, details add to the sensory impact. The audience must see, hear, and feel the meaning. In an abstract discussion, details must support the writer's points.

In order to improve one's writing, one must read it aloud often with the correct pauses, intonations, and rhythm. This reading must be done *as if performing it on the stage*!

Practice writing descriptive sentences. Rewrite them several times, changing the order of words, adding words, and reading them aloud each time while paying attention to the rhythm you obtain with each alteration. The good and bad versions of the sentence example about the lake will help you with this practice.

EXERCISE

Here is an exercise that will not only help others better understand what you have written but also help you improve your writing style.

- Step One: Choose a few medium length sentences from your writing and put them down separately on a piece of paper, leaving spaces between the sentences.
- Step Two: Tell a friend or a classmate that you are going to read sentences to her, and that after each sentence has been read, she will be expected to repeat it back to you exactly. She must focus on listening to you.
- Step Three: Read one sentence as you normally read aloud and wait for your friend to repeat it *exactly*. If he cannot do it at all, reread your sentence with correct pauses, tone, and rhythm and see whether this makes it easier for him to repeat it.
- Step Four: If your friend or classmate cannot repeat your sentence exactly, it may be for one of three possible reasons:
  1. He or she did not understand the task or did not pay attention.
  2. Your sentence was correctly written but poorly read.
  3. Your sentence was incorrectly constructed and punctuated, so it made no sense.

The second and third reasons are important feedback for you in your efforts to improve your writing. The third reason is the most important one.

Now that you understand the rhythm of a sentence and how it affects meaning and effective communication, learn to choose sentence structures that serve your meaning best.

5

WRITING CONTEXT MODELS

 ## AUTOBIOGRAPHY

Autobiographies are one of the most useful writing exercises because they require mostly description, a concrete writing style, and some reflection, which we all do about our experiences. Concrete descriptions are easier to write than abstract philosophical or argumentative pieces. Concrete writing uses a vocabulary that appeals to the senses. It makes use of many of the sentence structures learned in Chapter 1, answering the questions *who*, *what*, *when*, and *where*.

Autobiographies are also a cure for mental block. Students will always have something to say as they look back on their life. They also always automatically incorporate some level of reflection as they describe their reactions and feelings towards the major events of their life journey. As they reflect, they answer the questions *how* and *why*.

The autobiography writing exercise prepares students well for higher-level thinking skills development, a necessary step towards quality literature analysis and argumentation.

Everyone can write an autobiography because one knows enough facts of one's life to compose an interesting narrative.

The next twenty sentences provide a few models that can be used in writing the autobiography.

1. Born in Tennessee in 19xx, I became my parents' fourth and last child, a fact that influenced my entire life.

   _____

   _____

2. Born in a family of twelve, I learned early the value of sharing.

   _____

   _____

3. The first of three children, I soon took charge of my siblings who were much younger than I.

   _____

   _____

4. One of the best things that can happen in life is to have a happy childhood.

   _____

   _____

5. Looking back, I feel that my childhood was particularly lonely.

   _____

6. As a young child, I was so shy that I always tried to hide in my mother's skirts when taken to social gatherings.

   _____

   _____

7. My mother's father, a successful entrepreneur, was struck by a fatal illness when still young, and my grandmother was left to raise four children without the resources she was used to.

   _____

   _____

8. It was only later that I realized how much my parents loved each other.

   _____

9. The portrait that I have of her shows a young face with dark anxious eyes.

   _____

   _____

10. My sister's friend, Amy, had a brother whom I found handsome and exciting.

    _____

11. At the age of six, I fell in love.

    _____

    _____

12. When I think of it now, I realize that my brother was not at all as sure of himself as he appeared to be.

_____

_____

13. If I had not married, I most likely would have gone to college right after high school and become a nurse.

_____

_____

14. The plan for my life was now more or less established, but I had to make one more important decision.

_____

_____

15. Sustained by my desire to succeed in the profession of my choice, I embarked on a four-year term of study that put a strain on my life at home.

_____

_____

_____

16. When she died, a few years later, I felt I had lost one of my best friends.

_____

17. We had a lovely trip to Oregon, for the weather remained perfect without the frequent showers we were expecting.

_____

18. That my younger brother was a nerd, there was not a doubt in my mind.

_____

_____

19. To accomplish what my mother did, alone with five young children, required strength of character that I realized she had only when I became a mother myself.

_____

_____

_____

20. Of all the major events of my life, the death of my father when he was only forty-two years old threw me in despair and angered me for a long time.

_____

_____

_____

These twenty sentences represent a small sampling of sentence structures that are suitable for an autobiography. After practicing with them, explore the other structures learned in Chapter 3 and adapt them to the autobiographical content.

LITERARY ANALYSIS

Just as autobiographies help us reflect on our life journey, literature is the source of reflections by others on their own life journey and their choice of writing genres such as poems or novels to share personal opinions and feelings.

The skill of literature analysis is necessary for a college career, and it requires a specific approach to using language. Literature analysis must address both the content and the form of the piece under scrutiny. *Note that the present tense is always used in literature analysis.* This type of writing must include comments about plot, characters, and themes. It must also analyze elements of style such as the use of simile, personification, rhyme, and others.

Literature analysis writing concludes a process of reading, understanding, reflecting, and responding. It requires total immersion in the works that are read. When ready to respond, as in a dialogue with the author, one can look at the reading from many perspectives. They include biographical, psychological, historical, gender, and mythological investigations.

Literature always describes life, no matter what form it takes to do so. Responding to literature must include discussion of themes and issues that make one human. These issues can include such human concerns as home and family, love and its tragedies, birth and death, and culture and identity.

Here are a few samples of good writing for literature analysis:

1. Charles Dickens' *Great Expectations* tells the story of a young orphan, Pip, and his eventful life in Kent and later in London, England.

   _____

   _____

   _____

   _____

2. Pip falls in love with Estella and dreams of becoming wealthy so that he may be worthy of her.

   _____

   _____

   _____

3. In such a strict society as was Salem, one might picture a gray scene of cold, frowning faces somberly going about their daily toils.

   _____

   _____

   _____

4. However, through reading *The Crucible*, one might slowly form a vague, yet striking understanding of what it was really like to exist under such formidable and heavy laws.

_____

_____

_____

_____

5. In Arthur Miller's *The Crucible*, it is shown that personal and internal conflicts can manifest themselves in the persecution of others.

_____

_____

_____

6. Wang Lung-Wang, a farmer who loves his land, is the main protagonist in the book.

_____

_____

_____

7. We observe and judge his character as he struggles and thrives in pre-revolutionary China.

_____

_____

8. As Wang begins his special day, the characters are introduced within their own setting.

_____

_____

_____

9. This was exemplified in the literature of Kate Chopin who wrote *The Story of an Hour.*

_____

_____

10. In this short story, a woman, Mrs. Mallard, is told that her husband has just died.

_____

_____

11. While dealing with the shock of the revelation, she realizes that, beyond shock, she feels relief.

_____

_____

_____

12. It is the discovery of this feeling and the understanding that she finally has her life in her own hands that provides an enormous sense of empowerment.

13. The personal conflicts, which were exposed under the cover of a pointed finger, would not soon be forgotten in Salem.

14. In *Lord of the Flies*, William Golding illustrates that men turn to savagery once civilization is no longer present.

15. The conch, a perfect symbol of the ties to civilization, is destroyed; therefore, it symbolizes the loss of any remnants of society that had existed on the island.

16. In William Shakespeare's *Julius Caesar*, it is shown that the Romans are incapable of living in a republic.

17. As Marullus and Flavius search through the cheering crowd, they see the citizens of Rome anxiously praising Caesar who holds all power over their lives.

18. The reader discovers the letters written to Mrs. Saville by Walton and later reads the story of the voyage told by Walton; then, the reader hears the story of Victor Frankenstein through Victor's own narration, although Walton remains the storyteller.

    _____

    _____

    _____

    _____

19. This writing technique is sometimes referred to as *double frame*.

    _____

20. Upton Sinclair's *The Jungle* portrays confusion and chaos, which are both strikingly present in the novel.

    _____

    _____

    _____

21. One theme in F. Scott Fitzgerald's *The Great Gatsby* may be that focusing on a single goal blinds people to their life's other possibilities.

    _____

    _____

    _____

    _____

RESEARCH REPORTS

Research is an activity that must be approached scientifically and ethically. Its purpose is to search for new information and understanding and to answer questions with verified facts. Research must be conducted systematically, following strict methods, and sometimes it includes experiments. It always includes references to previous research. Pay attention to such references in the examples given in this section.

Many new social and business policies are created because of new facts discovered through research, so it is very important to take great care in collecting, analyzing, and interpreting the research data before drawing conclusions from it. For that reason, all research is concluded with a report that must conceal nothing of the entire research process. Research methodology is a specialized field. Once you have learned its process, you can apply it to many areas of knowledge such as sociology, psychology, medicine, and business.

The writing style used in research reports is different from other writing styles. Detail and precision are extremely important. It is acceptable to be redundant, and it is necessary to use an impersonal tone. For that reason, the passive voice is acceptable in research reports. It is also recommended not to use contractions. To write a good research report, you must know the principles of good writing as well as the principles and the terminology of the field you are researching.

Here are a few useful sentence models for the research report:

1. The purpose of this research project is to determine the feasibility of opening an Internet Café on the XYZ campus.

   _____

2. This research project is a summative evaluation of the home visits program at Louisville Elementary School.

   _____

3. Pretest and posttest questionnaires were given to parents to measure their perceptions of the school in three categories: Academic, Behavior, and Home-School Communication.

   _____

   _____

4. While there is considerable agreement on the benefits of bridging home and school, the methods used to reach that goal vary greatly.

   _____

   _____

5. It is uncertain whether this response is based on actual behavior changes or whether it reflects expectations.

_____

_____

_____

6. Durkheim (1951)* states that animals that have been abandoned by their owners often subsequently refuse food because of loneliness and misery.

_____

_____

_____

7. The first hypothesis in this research states that parents' involvement in their children's school experience always leads to higher test scores.

_____

_____

_____

8. Although communication between school and home has been identified as a first step towards increased parental involvement (Marcon, 1999)*, the nature of the communication style is vitally important.

_____

_____

_____

_____

9. Whether visits to parents in their home decrease their resistance to a relationship with the school cannot be determined.

_____

_____

_____

---

*This date and author's name represent examples of references to material used in research reports. They follow the American Psychological Association (APA) referencing style. They are examples of methods of inserting that information in a sentence. When you write research reports, you need to become familiar with all the requirements for citations and references from the style sheet required by your instructor.

10. Fifteen percent of all respondents indicated that they would come to the Internet Café and use its services on a regular basis.

_____

_____

11. A ten-question survey was created and distributed to a sample of thirty from the whole population of employees in the Information Technology Department.

_____

_____

_____

12. The researcher has discovered patterns of human behavior by studying the settings in which the culture is making itself known and by describing the perceptions of that culture's members.

_____

_____

_____

13. I collected data from three sources: face-to-face interviews, a mailed questionnaire, and previous research.

_____

_____

14. The following patterns and themes have emerged from this observational study.

_____

15. A minimum of 100 subjects will be solicited from each group to participate in the pretest data collection.

_____

_____

16. If subjects are no longer available for the posttest data collection, their pretest scores will be eliminated from the data to be analyzed.

_____

_____

_____

17. Two pilot studies were conducted as preliminary exploratory investigations.

_____

_____

18. The teaching variables for the first treatment group, or group receiving the experiment, included new terminology, definitions, and concrete examples.

_____

_____

_____

19. As part of the anecdotal data for this research, a teacher's report was included that described a successful experience with a student whose home the teacher visited.

_____

_____

_____

20. The survey distributed to employees generated nominal data from multiple choice questions and open-ended type interview questions.

_____

_____

_____

6

PARAGRAPH AND ESSAY TOPIC SUGGESTIONS

This text helps you write correct sentences. If you learn to consistently write a few correct sentences and build a sentence inventory, you will eventually be comfortable writing paragraphs and essays of any length. While you are learning correct sentence structures, quality is more important than quantity. Even if you write only five sentences on a given topic, you will feel gratified if they are all perfectly correct and have good rhythm. More to the point, you will have acquired techniques that you can repeat at will when writing on a variety of subjects.

Start with descriptive topics, move on to personal experience topics, and finally write about opinions and social issues. The following suggestions represent only a few ideas within these categories. You can easily think of similar topics and write on those or expand on one after you have written it. You might write several paragraphs on the same topic, exploring different perspectives. Most of all, write only about topics that you feel strongly about. That is the key to always having something to say and to be motivated to say it well.

DESCRIPTIVE TOPICS

1. Describe in vivid detail a favorite spot outdoors. It can be in the mountains, at the beach, in the country, or even in the city. Choose only one spot and describe its sounds, colors, smells, and atmosphere. You may add some details about the occasion or occasions that brought you there.
2. Describe in concrete detail your favorite activity when your time is your own.
3. Write your thoughts about professions that appeal to you.
4. Tell about your family group. Describe each member as you would a character in a book.
5. Describe a special event you attended like a wedding, graduation, or funeral. Make sure to include descriptive detail and also include a description of the activities involved.
6. Describe a neighborhood where you have lived.

7. Describe a work of art you have had the opportunity to examine. Identify the emotional impact it has had on you.
8. Describe in detail one of your trips to the local supermarket.
9. What is your place of employment like? Make it come alive for the reader.
10. If you have pets, describe them in detail. Tell what they look like and how they behave.

EXPERIENTIAL TOPICS

1. Write an autobiographical page. Use a free style; be creative. In other words, you might start with today and go back to the time of your birth, then jump to a special memory in between, and so on. If you prefer, use the chronological order. Most of all, make it a pleasant journey over the past and write it in perfectly correct sentences.
2. Describe what you consider the saddest event of your life and discuss the emotions it generated in you. If this event took place a long time ago, describe how your emotions about it might have evolved over time.
3. Tell about your first paid work experience. How did it come about? How old were you? How long did it last? What type of work was it? Where was it? How did you feel about it?
4. What was your worst or best educational experience? Write about it and give details about why it was so bad or so good.
5. Describe what growing up was like for you.
6. Describe the effect that music has on your life. Explain what types of music you like and dislike and why.
7. Stress is everywhere in our life. What are the most important stressors in your life and how do you cope with them?
8. Reflect on what motivates you the most to learn and accomplish your goals.
9. Discover and analyze your personal values. Do you think that values are only truly your own when you put them into practice?
10. To what extent have you experienced technology in your life?

OPINIONS AND SOCIAL ISSUES TOPICS

1. In your opinion, what methods are best to bring about good behavior in children?
2. Do you think that war video games are bad? Give your specific reasons.
3. The family structure is quite different today from what it was fifty years ago. Do you think that today's families that include many single-parent units can be as successful as those of the past? Do you think families of the past were happier than those of today, or do you think that the family structure and lifestyle are not important?
4. Discuss the influence of the media over what we eat.
5. What are the advantages and disadvantages of adapting to a new culture and language?
6. Take a position on the issue of using animals for research and defend that position in a well organized essay. Use very specific support for your views.

7. Some think that if the legal drinking age were lowered, binge drinking in college would not be as prevalent as it is now. Discuss your opinion on the subject. Support it with personal experience and logical reasoning.
8. Explain your views on the current influence by big corporations on government policy.
9. Explore the concept of *goodwill*. Define the word in your own way and discuss your views as to whether goodwill among people is still practiced today.
10. Do you think that sex education in schools has accomplished what it claimed to accomplish?
11. Is it more important for people to look after themselves first or should the common good be everyone's priority?
12. Some claim that rapid growth in population everywhere is the cause of many social ills. What are your views on methods of population control as practiced in some countries?

 # Index